A LAST JOURNEY

Ann Burnett

– LADYBUG PUBLICATIONS –

Published in 2024 by Ladybug Publications

Book design by Lumphanan Press
www.lumphananpress.co.uk

Front cover: Bill as a child admiring
his dad's first car in the 1950s

ISBN: 978-1-7385618-0-3

Printed and bound by Imprint Digital, UK

aboutDementia

PREFACE

This was a book I didn't mean to write, but like Topsy, 'it just growed'.

All through my husband Bill's illness I didn't have the time or the inclination to write, but after his death, when Marianne, a Ph.D. student, who interviewed me over six months as part of her research, sent me the transcripts of our conversations, I realised how much I'd actually forgotten about that terrible time. So I began jotting down bits here and there – the equipment that we'd had to acquire from Occupational Therapy; the struggles we'd had to get carers in to help with keeping Bill at home; his determination to keep moving – and eventually I came to the conclusion that I had the makings of a book. With all the articles and blogs I'd written about our travels and experiences, the diaries and letters I found and the thousands of slides and photos that were stored away in a large chest, it all gradually came together.

Too often tales of dementia focus on the problems of having the disease and ignore who the person is. One of the first things I did after Bill was diagnosed was to write a piece to give to the carers, the medics and the therapists who came in contact with him, to show who Bill was and what he'd done in his life. I wanted them to know that he was an educated, sporty, loving dad and husband, and not to define him by the effects of his illness.

This is only our story of dementia. Everybody dealing with this dreadful illness has their own version of it. But I hope readers enjoy reading our story and find this book useful.

ACKNOWLEDGEMENTS

My thanks are due to Dr Marianne Cranwell for providing the transcripts of our long conversations during her research for her doctorate, only part of which I have used here; to the Edinburgh Festival Theatre's Creative Engagement Team, especially Alex Howard, for getting me writing again and for putting a word in at the right place and time; to my editor, Gale Winskill for sterling work in sorting out all the bits and pieces of this book into a much more coherent whole; to Duncan Lockerbie and his team at Lumphanan Press for turning my manuscript into book shape.

My friends, Anne and Marjorie, provided Bill and me with so much love and support through truly difficult times, along with the members of the Dementia Singing Group and the staff at the Maitlandfield House Hotel.

Thanks are due to all the wonderful NHS staff that we came across in our journey, and to the innumerable carers who came into our home to help us.

To our sons, who were there for us during it all and who have continued to be there for me, along with their families, to provide love, laughter and IT knowledge.

And to Age Scotland – without your help and support, there wouldn't be a physical book, just a heap of tear-stained paper.

CONTENTS

INTRODUCTION

A LAST GIFT

My husband, Bill, and I imagined ourselves doddering along till we reached our eighties. Beyond that was a mist, fading away. But in our mid-seventies all that changed. Bill was diagnosed with dementia.

'I'm shocked,' he said to the consultant. 'I didn't think anything was wrong.'

But I knew. For several years something had been niggling away at me. Something wasn't quite right. Forgetfulness you can put down to ageing, but this was more than that. For our Golden Wedding in 2016, I'd bought printed badges bearing the names of all our guests, even having different-coloured backgrounds denoting whether they were family or friends. I thought it would benefit our guests, coming as they did from a variety of our interests and activities, even including Bill's new family members, who he'd only discovered the previous year. But really it was because Bill couldn't remember names.

I even moved us across the country to be nearer our sons 'just in case'. It took me until 2019 to persuade him to visit the GP and at least ask about his 'problem'.

What is dementia? Alzheimer's, the most common form, is what people usually think of when dementia is mentioned. But there are over 200 types of dementia and more may well be discovered. Every patient is different; they have their own unique symptoms and presentation of the disease. And the symptoms change and evolve as the disease progresses.

At the moment there is no cure. Every few weeks there is a media fanfare as yet another new miracle drug is claimed as the panacea for dementia. What they actually mean is that the drug might slow down the progression of the illness if it is caught early enough. A big *if*. Getting an early diagnosis is not easy these days. Doctors seem to be loath to actually do all the tests required to be able to say with any certainty that dementia is present. Is money and lack of resources the problem?

And dementia is terminal. It may be a long slow deterioration or, as in Bill's case, a rapid gallop towards the end. For him, there were almost exactly three years from diagnosis to death.

But instead, I'll focus on Bill's drive and determination to continue living, despite a doctor's prognosis which gave him only 18 months, as it was in Bill's nature to put his head down and charge at whatever he faced, however much it came back to knock him down again and again.

There are always two people involved in dementia: the sufferer and the carer. Much is spoken about help for people with dementia, but help for carers is much thinner on the ground. Although dementia sucks the personality out of the sufferer, it reduces the carer as well. Weeks, months, years of caring leave the carer in a state of limbo, neither a partner nor a professional carer, stuck between two states of being, unable to participate fully in the activities and hobbies they enjoyed before, with only the knowledge that ahead lies the death of the loved one and an emptiness beyond.

I joined Dementia Research and became part of a Ph.D. student's research. We met online roughly every two weeks for several months over summer 2020, with a final meeting in November 2020. She would start by asking how I was – a signal for me to let it all out. And I did. I spoke, I cried, I relived the previous fortnight and what had happened as I struggled to care for Bill. She recorded it, transcribed it and eventually, sent the transcript to me with a dedication to Bill.

I had tried to get as much help as I could, and went to as many dementia groups and meetings with Bill as possible. When Covid struck in March 2020, everything stopped. Online, I found a dementia group associated with the Festival Theatre in Edinburgh, who were trying to write a story with the help of a couple of playwrights. I joined them on Zoom for an hour every week while Bill was looked after by a sitter.

At this point, I had been writing for many years, including five years' worth of *Postman Pat* stories for a children's comic and over 100 radio and TV scripts for children's programmes on the BBC. I had written travel articles and short stories as well, and self-published a couple of novels which I hoped would make my fortune! But since Bill's diagnosis, I hadn't been able to write. I had neither the time, the energy or the inclination. I had frozen.

However, the Festival Theatre group asked me during Lockdown if I would write a wee piece on my experience of working with them for the *DementiArts* magazine that was put out online by the theatre – just 500 words. I managed to do it and then everything began to change. In 2021, I suggested to the magazine editor that I do a brief piece on the backstory of many of the dementia sufferers in our singing group, as I had been astounded to discover just what talented people they were, and what interesting and fascinating lives they had led before dementia got its nasty claws into them. There was a potter who had met the Dalai Lama, an acrobat who had been offered a job in Chipperfield's Circus, an RAF trombonist who'd played with Acker Bilk and performed at the Edinburgh Tattoo ...

My old writing skills, though terribly rusty, began to re-awaken. When Bill died in 2022, I already had a regular spot in the magazine writing the *Hidden Lives* column and the theatre offered me more work helping with their new podcasts. Other avenues opened. Because I was now considered to have 'lived experience' of dementia, I was recruited on to the theatre's focus group, planning how their dementia programme should go. I was also asked to join a University of Edinburgh research project into the arts and dementia.

Tentatively, I began to write again. Reading over the transcripts from my Zoom meetings with the student, I realised how much I had forgotten about my time spent caring for Bill and I didn't want that to happen. So I wrote about it in bits and pieces as the memories resurfaced. About the equipment the Occupational Therapy department had lent us, which took up so much space. About the punk physiotherapist who had phoned Bill regularly during Lockdown to see how he was doing. About the variety of women who came as carers and shared their lives with mine and Bill's. About the moments of joy and despair and sadness.

Gradually the pieces built up, until I realised I had the makings of a book. I mentioned this to my editor on the *DementiArts* magazine, Alex Howard, who happened to be going to a conference attended by representatives from Age

Scotland. He told them what I was doing, and as he said, 'Their ears pricked up'.

They offered to assist me with the book so I sent them the first draft of the manuscript and the result was a magnificent offer of funds to help get the book out there.

It's a last gift from Bill. If he hadn't had dementia, this wouldn't have happened. We'd have gone our doddery way, until perhaps something else took us.

Yes, I've lost him. And yes, I miss him terribly. But he's left me with the means to go on living a full life and hopefully, ensuring that his memory lives on.

PART I

GLOBE-TROTTING

– 1 –

CANADA, 1969

We had always planned to travel, and teachers in the late 1960s were wanted all round the world. We bought *The Times Educational Supplement* every week and scoured the ads for teaching positions. A couple of years living off a teacher's starting salary of £950 per annum had not been easy when Bill was finishing his degree. Canada attracted us due to the massive salaries they appeared to have, so that was our goal.

The interview was held in a bedroom at the Central Hotel, then the premier hotel in Glasgow. Even to our inexperienced eyes, it looked shabby and small, nothing like we had expected. Bill had already been for a preliminary interview that morning, in which the interviewer had been decidedly underwhelmed at the prospect of a Physics teacher with no experience. But when he discovered that there was a wife – me – with an interest in teaching pupils with special needs, his attitude changed.

Bill phoned me at the school at lunchtime – an unheard-of situation, only done in the case of emergencies or a death – and told me to meet him in Glasgow after school to present myself before this Canadian educator. He was from the Board of

Education for the City of Toronto. I packed up cards and charts I'd made to help my 'remedial pupils', as they were then called, and carted a bagful to the Central Hotel. He never looked at them, nor did I show them to him. After sizing me up (we discovered later he wanted to hear how Scottish we sounded and if we would be comprehensible to Canadian pupils), he produced contracts and signed us up on the spot. We would each be earning a salary greater than that earned by the headmaster of the large comprehensive school where I worked.

We were booked to sail from Liverpool on the *Empress of England* and coincidently were given the same cabin, C33, as our friends, who had sailed several weeks before us on the same deal. They'd had a marvellous time on board, enjoying fancy dress parties, cocktails with the captain, luscious dinners. We however, were seasick most of the way across, despite the fact that the captain had decreed that it wasn't rough enough to switch the stabilisers on.

We docked in Montreal and eventually arrived in Toronto late one evening, where we had to phone the deputy principal of Bill's school to come and pick us up and take us to the principal's home to stay. Mr Beckett had offered us accommodation but as he was away, he'd organised for the deputy to pick us up and take us there. The deputy wasn't sure of the address so we wandered along Mr Beckett's street after midnight, with the deputy peering through windows to see if he recognised the furnishings. I was sure that someone would call the police.

Eventually we got there and woke the principal's daughter who was having an illicit sleepover with her boyfriend, who only spoke French.

The next day we set off to find an apartment for ourselves. We checked out various high-rise blocks with no success until we visited our friends in their block, right across from Bill's school. There just happened to be an apartment that was about to become available, helped by a push from Mrs Scholtz, the caretaker's wife, who offered the occupant a deal he couldn't refuse. And after a thorough and much-needed clean it was ours.

However, we still had to stay with Mr and Mrs Beckett who had now returned, as we had no furniture. We had sold up before we left and what we had packed into the ship's hold hadn't yet arrived. The principal and his wife were a kindly couple who took us to a discount warehouse, where we bought a damaged table and four equally damaged chairs. Then we found Honest Ed's, a Poundland well before its time. Two camp beds, sundry wee coffee tables and a few lamps (our lamps were a different voltage and wouldn't work) were all we needed. Eventually, after a couple of wage cheques from our jobs, we splashed out and bought an 8-foot long Chesterfield, which I still have and which graces the lounge.

Our life in Canada had begun.

– 2 –

TEACHING, TRAVEL AND TEDDY KENNEDY, 1969–71

The Canadian system had three types of school at that time: *Collegiates*, which were the academic schools; *Technical Schools*, where the likes of building-trade skills were taught; and *Vocational Schools*, where the rest of the pupils went to be taught fast-order serving and other zero-hours contract jobs, as well as cookery, sewing and useful household skills.

Bill and his friends all taught in the Science Department at the collegiate across the road from our apartment, but because of my experience with the 'Remedial Classes', as they were then called, I was sent to a girls' vocational school in another part of the city where I was timetabled to teach Maths and Civics, of which I knew nothing. My first task was to explain the workings of the Toronto council system, elections for which were just about to be held. It wasn't to be the only school in my teaching career where I was faced with an unknown subject. In Australia, I was given a history class which would cover what was referred to as 'Aboriginal History' with a First Nations lad sitting staring up at me. Fortunately (or not), he was as ignorant of the subject as I was.

The girls in my Canadian school came from mainly immigrant backgrounds – Italian, Spanish, Portuguese. Their command of English was poor and they still adhered to their culture's customs. Most of them expected to be married shortly after leaving school. The rest were a mix of Indigenous Peoples or problematic white families.

Teacher assessments were common and were carried out by the principal or deputy principal. They would arrive in the classroom just as I was settling the class to begin my lesson and sit right at the back, notebook open to jot down their assessment of my work. I remember discussing, in a Scottish staffroom before I left, what a teacher should do when another teacher entered the classroom. The general consensus was to stop teaching, deal with the teacher's request, and not to start teaching again until the visitor had left the room – what happened in your classroom was your business, and yours alone.

So you can imagine my disquiet, and that of my fellow Scottish teachers, to discover that teacher assessment was part of the Toronto system and that we were required to sign a report of every assessment. That wasn't the only difference. There was no school uniform and a much more relaxed atmosphere between pupils and staff, even to the extent of them enquiring after my private life. I remember the teacher in the next room telling all her pupils about her family's difficulties in finding a house they liked in an area close to work, and what they could afford. She claimed it was a way of teaching the pupils about life in general and property in particular. Another would regularly take her class to her apartment (it was only across the road) and teach them how to bake, or chat about her choice of decor.

We, brought up in a system of the leather belt for bad behaviour and black university gowns (hiding our miniskirts), found it all very different.

As was our life outside work. The early 1970s were the days of flower power, of long floaty dresses, of musicals like *Hair*, which we went to see with our friends and were suitably shocked at the nudity, much to our husbands' amusement. We rented a cottage up on the lakes north of Toronto and spent Labor Weekend there with our friends, experiencing the Canadian love of the lakes and forests and the horrendous traffic jams on the 401 main route back to Toronto on the Monday night.

We bought a very large car, a Plymouth Fury, which had belonged to a teacher at my school. It had only been used to drive to school and back so its mileage was low. Bill took a couple of driving lessons as it was so different from anything he'd driven before in Scotland. We could pack our full-length skis into the back seat no bother!

Just after we returned from a New Year skiing trip to Quebec, we received news that Bill's mum had died suddenly. He immediately made arrangements to fly home, while his Head of Department insisted that Bill should do his lesson plans for the week he'd be away. It was a difficult time. I felt very lonely all alone in a new country while Bill was dealing with his loss back home.

But friends rallied round and Bill's dad flew out in the summer to spend time with us. We took him camping to Ottawa, where he decided that the pup tent we'd bought for him was too small and resorted to sleeping in the back seat of the Plymouth Fury.

My mother, who kept every letter I wrote to her from abroad, came out to Canada later that summer, and was appalled how skinny I'd become (I hadn't realised how much weight I'd lost with the stress of everything), and off we went camping again, with a bigger tent for her. This time we went to the Maritime Provinces, on the shores of the Atlantic. The national campsites were well run and maintained, and we were particularly enamoured with the Bay of Fundy site in New Brunswick, with its spectacular tides, stunning coastal scenery and abundant wildlife.

In the Easter holiday week of 1971 we rode an overnight Greyhound bus, first to New York, followed by Washington. Armed with a copy of Feldman's *New York on $5 and $10 a Day* and a similar book for Washington, we set out to explore 'the Big Apple'. According to the letter I wrote home:

> *We spent three days there, seeing the sights – the Empire State Building, the Statue of Liberty, Wall Street, the United Nations, the Rockefeller Centre, Radio City Music Hall (What a place! Holds 6,000; you pay $3 and you get a film plus a stage show, which is Billy Cotton at his best, 40 females high-kicking, corny songs about spring and birds, an orchestra which rises out of the pit, and an organ which plays during the intermission; potted palms all over the place, chandeliers, mirrors –pure 1930).*

The Twin Towers hadn't yet been built and when we did return to New York in 2002, they had already fallen.

We stayed in a clean but small hotel room in an out-of-the-way district where the elevator rattled its way to our floor and we looked across at another tenement building. We travelled by subway across the city, popping up out of whatever station was nearest to where we wanted to go.

We even went to Macy's department store where I bought a denim coat which I thought very fashionable and which lasted me for many years.

It was a busy few days before it was back on the bus and off to Washington. I wrote:

> *We toured the FBI, the Lincoln and Washington Memorials, the White House, where we saw the new Jackie Kennedy portrait [at that time, visitors were allowed in to tour round it], Capitol Hill, the place where they print dollar bills, the Custis-Lee mansion, the Pentagon (where we wandered past Melvin Laird's office – don't know whether we were supposed to be there, but we were lost), the Smithsonian Institution (saw the Wright brothers' plane, the Lindberghs' plane, the Apollo 8 spacecraft, a piece of moon rock – looked like a piece of clinker you get in the ash pan).*
>
> *But the highlight of the whole lot was our visit to Capitol Hill. We went on the guided tour and then we were told that if we got tickets we could get in to see the Senate in action. So we trotted along to the Sergeant at Arms, proved we were foreigners and got admission slips. We queued up, got in and 15 minutes later, the gallery was cleared to allow more people in. So we queued up again only to be told to leave a few minutes later as there was to be a full meeting of the Senate to vote on the SST bill (their version of Concorde). The public weren't allowed in – only the Senators' families (dressed up in their finery and fancy hats!), who had arrived in force even down to their grannies. However,*

the wee man at the door must have taken pity on us as he slipped us in between two senators' families. Talk about false pretences! However, it was well worth it as there was Spiro (Agnew) in the chair (he's really quite quiet and sober) and among the senators we spotted Goldwater, Humphrey, Kennedy, Taft, Muskie, plus a whole lot of others that Bill knew the names of.

After it was all over and we went outside, who should go dashing by but Spiro followed by his security guards. We were just recovering from that when Teddy Kennedy appeared to give a TV interview on the steps of the building.

We later spotted him waiting by the traffic lights to cross so I stood beside him while Bill snapped away. I was wearing my new Macy's coat in the photos! Someone said to us that we should say hello to him, but our Scottish reserve wouldn't let us and then the lights changed to green.

But itchy feet were beginning to disturb us again, this time due to Australian friends, Trevor and Sandy, who were over in Canada with us. Trevor was teaching for two years in the same department as Bill, and his tales of Aussie life had started us thinking. Especially, when Trevor told us of a startling offer the South Australian Board of Education was making.

– 3 –

SPORT

Bill was football mad as a kid, dashing out to play with a ball every free moment. There were several kids in the small enclave of hospital and farm labourers' houses built at the top of a hill and football was their game.

They played happily in whatever weather the Scots climate threw at them. But when they reached secondary school, Bill was disappointed to find that the sport they played there was rugby, in line with the middle-class, academic pretensions it had. Despite a former Rangers player and Scottish International being one of the PE teachers, football was never played, except informally in the playground.

So Bill played rugby despite being small and slight for his age and never developing the bulk that rugby required. However, he became good enough to become Vice Captain of one of the teams. But football remained his lifelong preference.

Later, he developed an interest in many other sports. In Canada, we joined a skiing club, taking our first steps as it were down a grassy hill in a Toronto park. It was autumn, or 'the fall', as they say, and the ground was carpeted with a thick layer of colourful slippery leaves. We tried out our new boots and skis on it, but it wasn't anything like the real thing. We had to wait till the first snowfalls further north of the city. Early every Sunday morning we would clamber on to a hired bus with the other club members and head out to the ski slopes. Ontario is not noted for its mountains, or even its hills, so the ski area consisted of a gentle downhill gradient, but to me and many other first-time skiers, it looked like Everest rising above us.

To get to the top of the hill in order to ski down, we had to master the ski tow. A continuous string of what looked like letter Js moved up and down the hill, and the trick was to grab one and hook it between your legs, keeping your skis in a straight line so you were pulled along the track upwards. My friend Margaret went ahead of me and grabbed the pole successfully and stuck it between her legs. Unfortunately, she thought you sat down on it and of course it stretched until she was sitting on the ground and the tow shuddered to a halt. After a quick lesson from an irate patrolman, she mastered the art and I followed behind. Bill and Margaret's husband, Walter, were helpless with laughter, they, of course, having sailed to the top where they were waiting for us.

I hated those Sundays. For a start I don't do early mornings, especially not on Sundays. But also, I'm uncoordinated, have a poor sense of balance and loathed PE at school, avoiding it as much as possible.

The husbands soon mastered snowplough turns and were zooming up and down, whereas Margaret and I quivered our way down inch by inch, with little kids screeching past us, waving their ski poles at us to get out of the way. The culmination of all those Sunday mornings was a week-long trip to Quebec City over New Year, where the skiing and the partying were meant to be good.

However, the bus taking the club members east across Canada hit the worst blizzard in living memory. We were stuck on that bus overnight in a line of traffic, waiting for the snowploughs to come through and clear the road. Eventually we reached our hotel where, to my delight, skiing was cancelled that day due to the high winds. Instead, we went for a walk through streets that were thigh-deep in snow in places, where snow-covered cars, stopped where they'd got stuck the previous day, proved another obstacle for the snow ploughs to overcome.

But Quebec City was beautiful. We climbed to the Château Frontenac and surveyed the snowscape below, which was nothing like the Glasgow slush of a snowfall back home. I could see why people wanted to get out in it and ski if that was the best means of transport. The next day, skiing classes began. The boys revelled in them, progressing through the classes like they were born to it. Margaret and I finished the week still in the nursery class and still teetering down the much bigger and longer slopes, while the boys tested their mettle on the black run.

Bill was a natural sportsman so when, in the summer, we were touring the eastern provinces of Canada and camping in the Bay of Fundy and I spotted tennis courts, I should have known better. I had batted a ball across the nets on the public courts in Glasgow's Queen's Park, couldn't serve or run after a ball, swiped randomly at the ball when it came near me and generally enjoyed the chat with my pals far more. I definitely shouldn't have said, 'Come on, I'll teach you how to play.'

Bill beat me 6–0 in the first set he ever played.

He continued to play when we lived in Australia, with the thermometer reaching near the dreaded 38° Celsius (100° Fahrenheit) in the summer. Beetroot-red, he played for one of the town teams every weekend and his competitive spirit came to the fore, as he was determined to beat his opponent, especially if they turned out to be one of his pupils or a pushy parent from one of the properties nearby. When we returned to Scotland he took a qualification as a tennis coach and, just to keep up his skills, became a ski-party leader, spending weekends up at Glenshee regardless of the howling winter storms.

But then he discovered his true love – running. It was at that time in the 1980s when running was taking off throughout the UK. Thousands of would-be runners bought running shoes and vests and pounded the streets morning and night. Bill and several other staff members used to go for a run in their lunch break – a far more generous break than teachers get now. They'd arrive back in school two minutes before the bell, change quickly and go off to their classes exuding strong odours of sweat all afternoon.

Bill soon extended his runs and his ambition. His first race was in Airdrie, a rather deprived Lanarkshire town. The race started off with a lap of the sports ground before heading out on to the streets. Bill was pleased he kept up with the front runners as they circuited the ground, cheered on by the spectators, but once they left the stadium, they took off at a far faster pace and Bill was left behind. However, he kept going, managing to complete the course, though only a few groundsmen were left in the stadium to cheer him in by the time he got back and crossed the finish line.

Marathons were his next goal and over the years, he competed in eight, including two London ones where I once I caught a glimpse of him on TV running alongside an infamous celebrity as the cameras focused on him. Numerous half-marathons, 10ks and

5ks had the family standing by the roadside on many a day waiting to cheer him on. He ended up with a massive haul of medals from all round Scotland and beyond, as well as photos of him crossing finishing lines with his time displayed above him.

– 4 –

CANADA TO AUSTRALIA, 1971

After two years in Canada, our itchy feet had only got itchier so instead of turning east and flying home to Scotland, we headed west and south and away down under. There was so much more we wanted to see, to experience and who could resist the enthusiastic South Australian who told us about the almond and orange trees in his garden, the barbecues out in the bush and the sun. The sunshine! We couldn't resist.

The South Australian Education Department paid for our tickets once we signed the contract (and who wouldn't want a free return ticket to Oz as long as you agreed to stay for two years?) I don't know if they were aware of what an 'open-ended' ticket meant. Or maybe they did and didn't care – an attitude of 'She'll be right, mate'. We could travel any route we wanted, stopping off as many times as we wanted, adding in extra flights and taking as long as we wanted, so long as we reached Adelaide in September. It wasn't till we scrutinised the contracts we'd signed that we realised that our salaries would drop to half of what we'd been earning in Canada. But hey ho, we were going to be seeing the world and experiencing another country! The travel bug had really gripped us.

So we set off across Canada by plane to Calgary and drove up to the Rockies, stopping at Banff and Jasper. We saw moose and mountain goats, and several bears at the roadside, where they knew to beg for food from the cars that had stopped. Then to Vancouver for a long weekend and a trip across to Vancouver Island before a short flight to Seattle where we picked up a plane heading north to Anchorage, Alaska. Everything there was so expensive, but we booked into a hotel and had a quick drink in the bar before bed only to discover that the waitress who had been very chatty, had told the DJ that there were two Scots in the bar. He immediately announced our presence and did an imitation bagpipe rendition. Cue a flurry of whiskies arriving at our table from the many customers there. We slept well that night.

The next day we flew even further north to an Inuit village, Kotzebue, at the edge of the Bering Sea, nearer to Siberia than New York. As the plane passed over the Arctic Circle, the pilot made the plane bump as if actually crossing a line, and then we headed further north to the very edge of the Bering Sea. The plane touched down on the gravel runway and cruised along the shore of the water before, thankfully, coming to a halt. Later, we received certificates celebrating our crossing of that particular imaginary line!

The first thing we saw in the town was a Kentucky Fried Chicken barrel whirling around on a pole. Even here, fast food had made its mark. Somehow we managed to attach ourselves to a tour group who were given a display of Inuit childcare (their babies tucked into their fur-lined hoods on their backs), singing and crafts, but we made our own way to the small museum in a hut in the town and spoke to a young Inuit girl who showed us school reading books written in their own language. I remember we bought a little ivory walrus made from an animal tusk which sits beside other souvenirs of our travels in IKEA's ubiquitous Billy bookcase in the lounge.

Although it was still summer, it was cold (8°C/47°F), with a strong wind blowing from Siberia just across the water, and we hadn't brought warm clothes with us. After all, we were heading for Australia, weren't we? So we were glad to fly back to the relative warmth of Seattle on the US west coast.

San Francisco was next on our agenda: Fisherman's Wharf, the cable cars and the Golden Gate Bridge; places and things we'd heard of, seen on TV or read about, but never thought we'd actually visit. Then to Los Angeles for the purpose of visiting Disneyland. It hadn't been on our original list of things to see, but our Australian friends, Trev and Sandy, had visited it on their way over to Canada, and insisted that we go – 'It's not just for kids. You'll have a great time.' We did.

This was in 1971, long before Disney World and the expansion of Disney parks around the world. We were enchanted. *It's a Small World*, *Mr Toad's Wild Ride*, *Space Mountain* – the whole park was like nothing we had ever seen before. We spent a glorious day there, going back again at night for the fireworks and seeing the whole site lit up.

For a bit more bling we went on to Las Vegas and walked the Strip in the evening. Slot machines were everywhere, even lining the corridors from the planes to the baggage carousel. We wandered into a couple of casinos, but as we had never played the games on offer, we were content to watch as others lost their money. Anyway, we didn't have that much to spend and certainly not to lose. I remember Elvis was singing at one of the fabulous night clubs.

Then a change of scene – the Grand Canyon in all its glory. We hadn't allowed enough time for a trip to the bottom, but we were content to travel around the rim and take in the spectacular views on all sides.

But time was creeping on and August was ending. We flew back to San Francisco where we picked up our flight to Sydney. At first, we didn't think we were going to be able to board, as the guy at the check-in desk held us back for quite a while. When he eventually beckoned us forward and finally checked us in with a nod and a wink, we realised that we had been upgraded to first class. This was 1971, remember, when flying was still quite a novelty to many people. First class was eye-opening. Real cutlery and meals on actual plates! Free drinks and linen napkins! Bill smoked in those days, little cigarillos, so when he took one out, the steward rushed over and lit it for him. We were loving it! But we literally came down to earth with a bump when the plane landed in Hawaii where we were bumped back into economy. But it was good while it lasted.

Our last stopover was in Fiji where, much to our surprise, we saw going through Customs ahead of us, the teaching couple we'd sat beside in the dining hall, those few times we weren't being seasick, on board the *Empress of England* two years earlier. They were also heading out to South Australia on the same deal as us – a free return ticket to Australia as long as we taught there for two years. The Australian guy who'd interviewed us in Adelaide had obviously crossed Canada recruiting more and more teachers.

Fiji was a tropical paradise and gave us a couple of days rest lounging by the pool and on the beach before heading for Sydney and then on to Adelaide.

When we at last arrived there, our Aussie friend Sandy's mum had come to greet us and say welcome to Oz, but the Board of Education representative, there to round up his new teachers, thought she was trying to poach us for the private sector and a bit of an altercation ensued until it was all cleared up. We had been promised two weeks' free accommodation before we were allocated our schools, so we were somewhat shocked to find ourselves in an immigrant hostel some way out of the city. It was also early spring and, quite frankly, chilly. Our light summer clothes were as much use there as they had been up in Kotzebue above the Arctic Circle.

Adelaide's immigration hostel was like going back 50 years in time. We had a room with a bed, shared toilets and showers, and we ate communally at long tables, in the middle of which were plates of buttered, sliced, white, pan bread. There was no heating so the new teachers from Canada (there was quite a crowd of us in among the 'regular' immigrants) headed out and bought two-bar electric fires to plug in, in our rooms. We immediately fused the electricity in the hostel and a loud Tannoy message in broad Aussie told us, in no uncertain terms, to unplug them immediately as they 'hadn't been tested for safety'. Considering they were straight out of the local Adelaide hardware store, it didn't seem a valid excuse.

We spent our two weeks' free accommodation finding our feet and trying to keep warm. One of the group, a wild Irishman with a Canadian wife, bought a wee, old car, the make of which totally escapes me, but I think it was a Morris Minor. It was a right banger, and every time he turned left, the door on the driver's side would swing open and bounce off the bonnet before swinging back and shutting again. Still, we saw quite a bit of Adelaide in it.

Our savings hadn't reached Australia yet and when we went to a bank to ask to borrow money so we could buy a car to drive down to the south-east of the state where we'd been posted, the manager was quite keen at first until he heard that our cash was due to arrive shortly.

'Don't be bloody stupid,' he said, or Aussie words to that effect. 'Just wait till it comes. No point is spending good money on a loan.' So he refused. I can't imagine a present-day manager saying that.

When the money arrived, we bought a wee red Renault that Bill carefully ran in at 40 mph (remember that process with a new car?) over the 250 miles down to Penola, our new home: 1,500 people, thousands of sheep and a far cry from brash, Americanised Toronto.

– 5 –

LIFE IN AUSTRALIA, 1971

Burns Night

The trouble was that, in Australia, we weren't Scottish enough. We had only been in Penola a week when a man called round to ask Bill to join the local pipe band. His face registered incomprehension when Bill confessed to being unable to play the bagpipes.

'But I thought you were Scottish?' he spluttered.

These inhabitants of the small South Australian town turned out to be more Scottish than us. Penola had been settled in the 1840s by waves of English, Irish and Scots immigrants drawn to the offers of free land. Alexander Cameron from Lochaber was the first, setting up Penola Station in 1844. Another, John Riddoch from Turriff, had first gone to the goldfields to make his money. In 1861, he had come to the area where he had bought 35,000 acres. He had recognised the importance of the red earth – the *terra rossa* – for growing grapes, and encouraged the settlers to plant vines. His foresight ensured the prosperity of the area and Coonawarra wines are now world-class.

But there was a price the settlers had to pay. The older part of the graveyard in Penola was filled with the graves of those first immigrants; young men and women who had come from Tain and Aberfeldy, Dumfries and Lewis; their infant children, of whom there were many; and their older children, who had managed to survive the difficult first five years only to die of some fever, or snakebite, or accident with the cattle. It made hard reading. Some names were still evident in the town – McLeod and MacKay, Meikle and Burns. Their descendants still lived in Penola, and if perhaps not wealthy, then managing to live a reasonable life far beyond the dreams of their ancestors.

They kept up the old traditions too. Or at least, they had versions of them, passed down through generations and adapted and modified to meet the circumstances.

So it was that we found ourselves at a Burns Supper one 30 November. They are usually held to celebrate Scotland's national poet on or near 25 January, Robert Burns' birthday. Instead, the inhabitants of Penola held it on St Andrew's Day.

It was early summer and already the temperature had risen into the mid-thirties Celsius (nineties Fahrenheit) and stayed there well into the evening. Bill, despite his musical inabilities, had been asked to do the 'Address to a Haggis' – the Burns' poem written to celebrate the poet's favourite dish. Bill wasn't keen. He had never been to a Burns Supper. He had never read much Burns apart from having to learn 'To a Mouse' for a school poetry competition in Primary 5. He had left Scotland to get away from the kitsch of tartan and shortbread. I had to dragoon him into accepting.

The evening began in the local Church of Scotland with communal singing. We started with 'The Bonny Banks of Lock Lo-mont' followed by 'It's a Long Way to Tipperary' and climaxing with 'Danny Boy'. It was eclectic and surprisingly good fun given the setting. We then retired to the church hall, where Bill was to do his piece. Dressed as he was in his best Canadian, pale-blue Zoot suit, he was only slightly put out to see that he was the only male not in the kilt. He didn't possess one. He had never even hired one. He had no intention of ever wearing one.

However, he did his part with remarkable aplomb. The piper led the procession in – was that the job they had hoped he'd fill? – and the haggis followed in tartan splendour on a silver platter. It was set in front of Bill and he recited the verses with the assistance of the crib cards I had prepared for him.

Fair fa' yer honest, sonsie face,
Great Chieftain o' the Puddin'-race!
Aboon them a' ye tak yer place,
Painch, tripe or thairm ...

'What on earth does it all mean? I don't understand a word of it,' he'd said, when I handed the cards to him a few days before.

'Just learn it, will you?' was my unsympathetic reply.

Bill stabbed the haggis with the kitchen knife provided, which went in with a satisfying *splurch*, and duly mangled the beast. It was then taken away and, to our surprise, the buffet began: sandwiches, chicken legs, sausage rolls, salad – all followed by the best Australian pavlovas, sickly sweet and soft, and drenched in cream and fruit.

Then came the haggis. On cocktail sticks. And mercifully in bite-size pieces. After the tooth-rotting pavlova, it tasted ... well, out of place. Some of the guests refused to touch it, treating it like some outlandish foreign muck. As it is. In Australia at any rate.

The night gave us many a laugh in the forthcoming months. How those daft Aussies didn't know how – or when – to hold a Burns Supper. How they couldn't tell the difference between the Scots and Irish heritage. Conveniently, we forgot our own ignorance and denial of Scotland.

Time, maturity, whatever, have lessened our ribaldry, have given us an understanding of what it meant. It wasn't a celebration of Burns, or of Scotland. It was an act of remembrance of all those names in the graveyard. Of James McLeod from Lewis, Robina Meikle from Tain ... of countless, nameless, infant children. Of all those brave souls who had set out from Scotland to face the unknown, who had left behind family and friends, knowing that the chances of ever seeing them again were virtually nil. Who were prepared to face great hardship in order to attempt to forge a better life for their families.

They had a long hard struggle in a strange environment, where nothing existed that they were familiar with. No identifiable trees or animals, save those they brought with them. No rains or mists or mountains, or stretches of open sea or lochs. No blackbird song or gulls' cry. No Gaelic, save their own speech. No tales but those they told themselves.

Is it any wonder they clung to the familiar traditions and habits? That they tried to keep burning that which identified them as Scottish?

So on each Burns Night, I raise my glass to them, to those pioneers who showed such bravery and strength and resolution. I celebrate the character of those long-dead Scots and the legacy they left behind.

Slainte. Good on you, mate.

– 6 –

MAUREEN AND BARRY

We met Maureen and Barry when Maureen came to teach for a term at our country school in Australia. Barry was a wool classer accompanying the shearers on their runs through the countryside, stopping at properties to shear the many thousands of sheep on each.

They lived in a caravan that they towed behind their ute, and parked up wherever was suitable. If there wasn't a school nearby for Maureen to teach in (she was a science teacher and in great demand), then she would act as the shearers' cook, turning out vast meals to satisfy the hunger of the men after their eight-hour shift.

At the end of their stint in the south-east of South Australia, they headed off up north for another shearing run that they'd been contracted to do and then made their way to Alice Springs for some free time. They suggested that we join them, so at the next school break, we flew up to Alice where they met us and took us to where they were camped. The caravan had been left in the town as where they were heading, the roads were not suitable for such a vehicle. In other words, we were going off road and camping in the bush.

The ground was part sandy, part stony with roots and debris, not exactly comfy, but Barry showed us how to dig out a hollow for our hips as a bed. What really ensured a good night's sleep was the liquor supply they carried in the back of their ute; flagons of Aussie red and white wine, sherry and port, liberally dispensed every evening with the food Maureen cooked over the campfire. She was a good cook and could serve up delicious meals from a cast-iron cooking pot resting on the glowing hot coals. It was quite magical sitting there of a night, only the fire giving us any illumination and the stars of the southern sky clear and twinkling above us, our stomachs full and our heads swooning gently from the booze. No wonder we slept well.

They took us to Uluru (previously, Ayers Rock) which we climbed, this being the days when such a thing was allowed. Nowadays, there is much more respect for Aboriginal sacred sites and this is now not allowed. Then to Kings Canyon, where hidden among the bluffs of red rock, is a pool of clear water, an oasis among the scrubby desert all around. But we weren't the first there that day; a busload of schoolgirls had arrived early that morning and were swimming happily in the water or perched on top of the rocks around the edge like mermaids. They were on a tour of the outback, staying in the remote homesteads, before returning to their Sydney homes.

Maureen and Barry would turn their hand to any exploit that took their fancy and were very keen that we join in. So the next school holidays found us up on the Murray River at Loxton for the Loxton Fair. They had been contracted to run a Billy Tea and Damper stall to sell to the visitors. Barry did a great line in making billy tea. First, get the campfire going and set a billy of water on to boil. When it's boiling, add a few tea leaves and then swing the billy can in circles with arm outstretched to impress the gawping visitors. Pluck a few gum leaves from the nearest eucalyptus tree (there are always plenty of them about), add to the billy and leave to stew for a few minutes before serving in paper cups to the grateful customers.

Maureen was just as theatrical. She would mix flour and water and a good pinch of salt in a bowl, before kneading the mixture and shaping it into a round, placing it in a cast-iron cooking pot (previously used for our meals in the outback), and setting it on another campfire to cook. It didn't take long. Meantime she prepared another damper for cooking. The first damper would be tipped out of the pot, slightly golden on top and like a large scone. It smelt delicious, as the watching crowd appreciated. Eating it sliced and spread with butter, along with billy tea, was really living the Aussie dream! The crowd couldn't get enough of it.

So what was our role in such a venture? We served the long queue which formed, and took the money. It was a very busy day and the crowd didn't seem to bother about the wait. While Maureen and Barry looked the part (they did normally: Barry with his scruffy beard and battered hat and shorts; and Maureen looking every inch a pioneer woman), the people – that is, us – serving sounded as Glasgow as they come. There was no point in trying to pretend to be a genuine 'Ocker', as you can take the girl out of Glasgow, but not the Glasgow out of the girl, as the saying goes.

'Ann and Bill!' came the cry and we paused in our customer service to find our headmaster and his wife staring in astonishment at us. They were up on the river visiting family and had never expected to see staff members engaged in alternative employment. But there was no contest. Our takings for the day, less the cost of ingredients and then divided by four, only got us a beer in the local pub.

Then there was the time Maureen and Barry purchased an old lifeboat, did it up, made it waterproof at least, installed bunk beds and basic cooking facilities, and set off to map the Murray River. It floods yearly leaving sandbanks and bends where there weren't any before, which makes sailing up and down difficult for pleasure steamers and craft to negotiate. Their idea was to produce up-to-date charts of the river so that boats wouldn't get stuck on the many snags that had appeared after flooding.

So of course we had to join them to see what they were up to. It was a pretty small boat but fitted the two of them just fine. With the four of us it was a squeeze. Two had to camp on the bank each night while two (us) slept in the narrow bunks. Toilet facilities were basic. If you couldn't jump on to the bank and find a spot among the trees, then there was a bucket placed in a recess below Barry's feet as he steered along the river. Only used if absolutely desperate.

After the flooding, the river was brown with silt and mud, but as the weather was hot, it was glorious to slip over the side and into the cooling waters. Wielding a net allowed us to catch yabbies, a freshwater crustacean prevalent in the Murray, which when cooked with garlic and fresh herbs, made a very tasty meal. It was only later on, slightly further upriver, that we spotted that the submerged building we had sailed past had a sign which read *Gents Toilets*. Fortunately we suffered no ill effects.

They published their charts and made many return trips to the Murray as, each year, the snags and sandbanks moved their positions. You can see their charts at **rivermurraycharts.com.au.**

– 7 –

AUSTRALIAN WILDLIFE

Yes, there are snakes and poisonous spiders and loads of other dangerous animals in Australia, and when we arrived in Penola, the locals were keen that we got to understand the risks involved. The town was surrounded by farmland, mainly grazing for cattle, and tiger snakes were plentiful in the fields. They are extremely venomous and hospitals carry antivenin for anybody who has the misfortune to be bitten.

So, sitting in the local pub one night, the farmers regaled us with advice on what to do if we found a tiger snake in our vicinity. A couple of naive Scots were just the audience they needed.

'Get a broom and hit it on the head,' said one.

'Go for the head! Grab the tail and crack the snake like a whip,' another advised, while warning us not to swing the snake too far back, 'as it could bite you on the bum'.

Shades of Loch Ness Monster tales and haggis hunts!

We headed home that night determined to avoid all snakes if possible. We settled into our new life, enjoying the sunshine and our new home. It was a semi-detached bungalow, just built, with a large back garden filled with 3-foot-high Phalaris grass. We would have to cut it down if we wanted anything else to grow there, but in the meantime we had other priorities.

I was hanging out my washing one day on the whirly in the middle of this grass when I noticed the stalks moving. It was a calm day so there was no wind. Mesmerised, I stopped pegging out the clothes and watched. The wave came towards me and suddenly a large reptilian head burst out and flicked its forked tongue at me. I fled into the house, scattering knickers and socks everywhere.

'Bill!' I yelled. 'Snake!'

He peered out of the window at the creature still flicking its tongue in the garden. 'If that's the head,' he said, appalled, 'there must be another 6 feet in the grass.'

Picking it up by the tail and flicking it like a whip was not an option. The broom was handy. So clutching it firmly, we edged out. The creature stared at us, casually scenting the air with its forked tongue. Grasping the handle of the broom, Bill raised it high and *thwack*! brought it down on the reptile. It flew up into the air, revealing itself to be only a couple of feet long and possessing four short legs. It was a harmless stumpy lizard which no one had bothered to mention to us.

Another time, one of Bill's colleagues was on the local golf course, nine holes of scrubland with not a spot of green to be seen. He was practising his swing and drove a powerful stroke into the air, accompanied by a tiger snake clinging to the end of his club. He gave up the game after that.

But we rarely saw any snakes: a long grey one slithered across the road in front of our car in Queensland; in Florida, one slipped past Bill while he was sitting reading the paper outside our mobile home and made its way into the ladies toilets; and when visiting the late Steve Irwin's Australia Zoo, in Queensland, we had the pleasure of holding a python, surprised by its smooth silkiness and generally harmless demeanour.

However, Barry, our Australian friend, was bitten by a tiger snake while stepping over a log near the banks of the Murray River, where they were living on their boat while mapping the river snags. The snake got his ankle leaving two tiny pricks and a drop or two of blood. But they were well-prepared and knew what to do. Maureen applied a pressure bandage to prevent the venom spreading along his leg and then they phoned for an ambulance from the nearest house (this being before mobile phones). Within an hour and a half, Barry was in hospital being given antivenin.

But it took many weeks before the wound healed, the pain had gone and he was able to walk comfortably again. Had he received a full dose of venom from the snake, then the outcome would have been fatal.

– 8 –

HOME TO SCOTLAND
THE OTHER WAY, 1975

We still had the other half of our original open-return ticket home. After four years in Australia we thought we'd better use it and so we planned a trip back to the UK, but heading westwards.

We spent three days on the Indian–Pacific train, crossing the continent from Sydney to Perth. We had a compartment with seats that folded into beds at night and a tiny cupboard of a bathroom. You could either use the toilet, wash your hands or have a shower, but only one thing at a time as everything folded into something else, or was covered by another porcelain doodah.

But the food was good, plentiful and helped pass the time.

Crossing the Nullabor, the desert-like plain along the edge of the Great Australian Bight, the railway line is empty, straight and runs from South Australia into Western Australia for over 600 miles, with scarcely a bend and only scrub and scrawny plants to see. Few people live here.

The train stopped occasionally at railway cottages to drop off supplies and the whole family would come out to see the train and the bemused passengers at the windows. Some energetic passengers climbed down to stretch their legs, but there was not much to look at and nowhere to go. I was full of admiration for the railway worker and his wife and kids who lived there, having to totally rely on themselves and the supplies the train brought every few days as it passed. There was no other company for them or the children, school was over the radio – the School of the Air – and if anyone was sick or hurt then it was up to the Flying Doctor service to come to their aid.

I remember seeing my first black swans in Perth. It was a thriving metropolis compared to the tiny settlements, even mining towns like Kalgoorlie that we passed through, but nothing like it is today. When we returned to the city 40 years later, it was huge and totally unrecognisable.

We were only in Perth for a couple of days before we were finally going to leave Australia and fly out to Mauritius. The travel agent in Adelaide had never heard of the island, and neither had we, but we wanted to stop off somewhere in the Indian Ocean and it was a toss-up between the Seychelles (or 'Seashells', as she pronounced it) and Mauritius, and Mauritius won, though the plane did land at the Seychelles on its way to Nairobi.

Our leaving Australia was pretty emotional. We didn't know if we'd ever be back or if we'd see any of our Aussie friends again. We'd avoided meeting up with some of them in Adelaide, as we were too embarrassed about our tears to do so. Partings were always difficult for us both. When the train pulled so slowly out of Central Station in Glasgow when we'd first set off on our travels in 1969, I remember my mother stoically holding back her tears and not meeting my eye, whereas Bill's mum's face was twisted in agony. That was the last time we saw her, as she died less than six months after we left. What we didn't understand was that she'd already had another son who had left with his wife and young children for overseas – for Australia in fact – and here was her other, much younger son, doing the same. Over 40 years later, we found out her secret.

But back to Mauritius. At that time, 1975, it was really unspoiled. Most tourists came from Africa for honeymoons or special occasions. We had a room that led directly on to the beach; as idyllic a setting as we'd ever seen. We were surrounded by lush gardens where every day, sweepers would brush away any fallen leaves or petals. We hired a car, a Mini, and drove around the island, visiting the capital Port Louis and Curepipe, where I bought a sari, there being a large Indian population. On one of our drives, we stopped outside a shack built from corrugated iron and whatever else the inhabitants could find. The owner came out and introduced himself – Olivier – and his wife. They ushered us inside and proudly showed us their prized possession, a transistor radio. Bill quietly slipped him some money to thank them for their hospitality.

Trying to leave Mauritius was difficult. It took five trips to the airport, five attempts to clear Customs and Duty Free, five exit stamps in our passports, all in the space of three days. We were a group of about 30, all attempting to travel to Nairobi in Kenya, with Kenyan Airways. There were plenty of excuses: the plane hadn't arrived in Nairobi from its previous destination; the plane had a technical fault; the weather was too stormy for it to fly; the pilot had to be replaced ... None of it reassuring. The staff tried to act normally, bussing us to and from the airport and settling us in a different hotel every night. We found it an inconvenience, and the family with a baby had great difficulty finding suitable food for her at one Indian hotel we stayed in, curries being the staple food on offer. Another passenger, an elderly lady trying to visit her son in Kenya, collapsed in the queue waiting to board the non-existent plane and had to be given some medical attention. She recovered and was able to join the flight that appeared one morning to rescue us and fly us off to Kenya.

No, it wasn't Kenyan Airways, but good old BOAC – the British Overseas Airway Corporation. A cliché of a British flying officer dressed in white shorts and epauletted short-sleeved shirt, long socks and peaked cap arrived at the hotel at six o'clock one morning with a bus to take us to the airport.

'Just take your time, ladies and gentlemen,' he said in plummy, upper-class tones, 'The plane will wait.' We dressed hastily, packed and jumped on the bus. Sure enough, there was the plane, complete with crew and ready to go. We didn't mind sitting squashed up next to the toilets. We were actually leaving.

'Where have you been?' was my brother's greeting in the Nairobi terminal when we eventually arrived.

After the heat of Mauritius, Nairobi, although on the Equator, felt cool and fresh, being several thousand feet above sea level. We didn't stay there for long. My brother, Alan, was a lecturer in Geography at the university, but it had just been closed temporarily due to riots which had broken out, so he had no lectures scheduled.

'We'll go camping in Amboseli Game Reserve,' he suggested. 'I'll borrow the department's Land Rover.' He also found another lecturer willing to come with us. Gary had come up from the country to give a lecture, armed with only his lecture notes and a toothbrush and wearing his best tweed jacket, but undaunted, he agreed to come on a five-day camping trip to the game park.

It was quite an experience camping out in tents borrowed from the Geography Department. One morning I peeked out of the tent opening to find a pile of still gently steaming elephant dung a few feet away. I hadn't heard a thing as the large bulk of an elephant had walked close by and deposited a special greeting.

The Masai were everywhere, the young men dressed in nothing but their dark-orange robes, all carrying spears and wearing colourful bead necklaces and bracelets. Empty film cartridges (remember, this was long before digital cameras and phones) were the decoration of choice for the pierced holes in their earlobes. But they were camera-shy … until you flashed some money. But we were nearing the end of our trip and money was far from plentiful, not that we ever had that much to spend, most of it having been transferred home in the hope it would be enough for a deposit for a house there.

We saw some animals like elephant and buffalo, monkeys and deer, but no big cats which was disappointing, though on our last night there, we certainly heard them. Our subtle attempts to sneak photos of the Masai men were futile. Either they noticed what I was up to and turned away, or demanded money, or they were too far away to be much more than a dot on the film.

As we were leaving Amboseli, the Land Rover broke down. We had paused for another last attempt to take pictures of Masai, but the car refused to start again. We pushed it to the top of a rise overlooking the Rift Valley, and there we sat for hour after hour while Alan attempted vainly to get it going again. Gary, a Swahili speaker, was dispatched on a passing beer lorry, carrying my Automobile Association membership card to phone the AA – a desperate idea, but what else could we do? We were miles from the nearest garage. The Masai children became more confident around us, seeing as we were going nowhere, and surrounded us, marvelling at our hairy legs and whitish skins.

One emboldened young warrior, clutching his spear, the shaft of which had *Made in Birmingham* stamped on it, jokingly (I hoped) offered my husband two cows for me. Being tall and skinny, I was the perfect shape for a Masai wife. Fortunately, Bill refused, explaining (also jokingly, I hoped) that he couldn't take the cows home on the plane.

The day inched past. A few beers and a couple of over-ripe mangoes were all we had left from our supplies. A bus stopped and out stepped Gary.

'Well, I did phone ...' he said.

The African night grew closer. Suddenly, there was a commotion.

'The local chief's son is coming,' Gary translated.

Sure enough, a striking young man appeared from the bush and beckoned us to follow. Alan stayed with the car – 'There won't be anything left if I don't.' – while Gary, Bill and I followed the Masai through the bush to the village of round huts made from adobe and surrounded by a thick hedge of acacia thorns – 'To keep the lions out,' Gary explained helpfully.

He also told us how the Masai liked to add fresh blood from a cow to their milk. They would pierce the cow's jugular and let the blood spurt into the milk before sealing up the hole for the next time. The young man took us to meet his father, the chief, who, sure enough, ordered a cow to be milked for us. The warm milk was poured carefully from the gourd into an empty Coke bottle, which had been washed out at their tap and, minus any trace of added blood, we were sent on our way back to the car which was still happily intact.

We sat on the bonnet in the blackness, listening to the sounds of an African night. Lions roared, fortunately from a distance. Other less recognisable grunts and chirrups broke the silence. We whispered as our tummies rumbled from hunger. Then, far below us in the valley, a tiny yellow light flashed. And flashed again. We watched as it crawled its way towards us. The AA had arrived.

Cairo was relatively uneventful after Kenya, though we were treated by Abdul, our guide, to a trip inside a pyramid at Giza. The passages were steep and narrow and led into small rooms where empty sarcophagi sat. To say it was claustrophobic is an understatement. I think we were waiting for Adbul to demand an extra payment to lead us back out, but he was not a greedy man and soon we saw blue sky again.

We arrived back in Glasgow on a chilly June day, it having snowed the day before. That's Scottish weather for you!

– 9 –

SCOTLAND, 1975–2018

Although, after we returned to Scotland, we did normal things like buying a house and having children, our wanderlust never really left us. But it wasn't till the boys left babyhood and our bank balances recovered once I started writing and selling my work, that we had enough cash, just about, to take us all to Florida's Disney World.

We did it as cheaply as we could; a charter flight found from Teletext, leaving from an obscure airport at an unearthly hour and refuelling in Bangor, Maine (not the Irish Bangor as I initially thought), and finding accommodation in a mobile home park, home to an interesting selection of Americans. But we toured the parks, bought new trainers at half the price of UK ones and thoroughly enjoyed ourselves.

In 1993, we swapped houses and cars with our friends Istvan and Eva in Toronto (Istvan and Bill had taught together when we lived in Canada). They and their three kids drove around Scotland before heading to Europe and their home country of Hungary, while we packed their van full of the camping gear we found in their basement and set off with our boys across Canada to the west coast. We had forgotten how vast Canada was – it took us three days to get out of Ontario!

And camping was problematic, at least for us. The boys were much more adaptable. It was almost 20 years since we'd camped in Amboseli and our bones had aged somewhat. My airbed burst, it was really cold at night so we had to buy extra blankets at the Hudson Bay Store, and despite them, we still had to use vast quantities of daily newspapers to wrap round the sleeping bags. Noisy rustling at night occurred any time anybody moved, but it worked. The only one warm enough at night was Christopher and that was because he'd commandeered the only heat pad. In the end, I protested and we decided we could afford to sleep in a cheap motel every third night.

We drove straight across Canada, stopping, among other places, at Spirit Sands, part of the Spruce Woods Provincial Park in the middle of the prairies. As Bill described it in his part of our diary,

> *This is a sacred Amerindian site of rolling sand dunes that could be in the Middle East if you didn't know better (we were in Manitoba). After a 10-mile hike through the dunes, we drove on to Indian Head and a cheap motel – the 'Bates Motel' we named it.*

The bathroom floor was soggy and sank under our feet, the beds were saggy but fortunately clean though very shabby, and the local Hell's Angels chapter was staying next door, but for CAD$40 a night, we could just afford it.

We found a modern campsite with clean toilets and showers in Banff in Alberta and stayed several days there. We took the chairlift up Sulphur Mountain, as well as visiting the Athabasca Glacier again, where we could see the extent by which it had retreated since we had last visited on our way to Australia in 1971. And that was before we became aware of global warming.

On the border of Alberta and British Columbia is the Great Divide where Kicking Horse Pass, at over 5,000 feet, provides a route through the Rockies. Here, Divide Creek forks into two branches, one flowing on to the Pacific Ocean while the other flows east to the Atlantic.

From there we headed south into the USA and the incredible state of Montana and Glacier National Park. We drove up the Going-to-the-Sun Road to Logan Pass (6,646 feet). Bill wrote in our diary of the trip:

> *The drive was interesting and spectacular. In fact there were so many fine views that we had reached saturation point by Logan Pass. The pass is only open from the end of June till early October. In winter it is covered in 80 inches of snow. The Rising Sun campsite turned out to be one of our better ones. It was open, sunny and quiet. It also had a spectacular view of the mountains.*

But Beartooth Pass from Montana into Wyoming and Yellowstone National Park was even more stunning. I wrote:

> *An extraordinary drive over Beartooth Pass rising to almost 11,000 feet. At 9,000 feet we stopped at the Top of the World Store (no phone, no electricity) to buy postcards. Amazing number of people there. The road was winding and like the train routes in Switzerland, you could see the cars zigzagging up the mountain. We stopped at the summit for photos and then on the way*

down the brakes burned hot and we could smell the rubber, but we made it.

Yellowstone National Park in Wyoming was also pretty spectacular with its gurgling mud pools, bears and buffalo and Old Faithful geyser, while further on, we went on various tours about Custer's Last Stand at Little Bighorn, including one from the Lakota tribe's point of view, and Mount Rushmore with the heads of the presidents, before we headed back to Toronto and then home.

After Bill retired and the boys had finished their education, the two of us took off again. Oh, the bliss of not having to travel during the school holidays! A trip back to Australia (more of which I've described in the next chapter) and then New Zealand. Other years we visited China, South Africa and met up with family there, then Japan (amazing toilets!), Mauritius (40 years after our first visit), Florida (where I fell and broke my hip and experienced US health care: 'Can I see your credit card, ma'am?' while lying immobile on the ground).

Our last trip abroad was in 2018, to Iceland, to our older son Ronan's wedding, at the foot of a glacier. A fitting finale to all our travels.

– 10 –

RETURN TO AUSTRALIA, 2009

In 2009, after Bill retired, we made our first return visit to Australia, hiring a camper van and setting off to visit our former home and the area round about. It was July and mid-winter, when temperatures can get down below freezing in the south-east of South Australia, which we should have remembered after living there for four years. We were cold at night in the thin sleeping bags supplied by the rental company, but we just wore everything in bed that we'd brought with us and hoped that we wouldn't have to get out of the camper van in the night. This is what I wrote about our visit:

Coonawarra Reds and Giant Kangaroos

'Are you sure they're extinct?' I said, peering round anxiously as we set up the van for electricity and water.

'You've had too much red wine,' replied Bill.

Midway on the long road between Melbourne and Adelaide is the Limestone Coast of South Australia, an area which deserves to be visited but which is often bypassed. It is home to some of

Australia's finest red wines, as well as to one of the most amazing fossil finds ever.

Approaching the Limestone Coast, the land becomes red and glowing, similar to the tracts of land in the outback. But this is fertile land, originally used for sheep and cattle grazing. Its name derives from the bed of limestone which underlies the red earth and provides excellent drainage for the area. It is dotted with small towns, the names of which come from ancient Aboriginal languages: Kalangadoo and Nangwarry, Penola, Coonawarra and Naracoorte.

When we had lived in Penola, just south of Coonawarra and Naracoorte, 35 years earlier, the area was just beginning to bloom. Now we were back, jaws dropping at the changes we saw.

Coonawarra is now one of Australia's finest wine-producing regions. The name means 'honeysuckle' in the local Aboriginal language and the area's potential for producing grapes was first recognised by a Scot, John Riddoch, in the nineteenth century. He had arrived in Australia in 1852 and had been a successful goldminer. He made even more money by investing in a store in the Ballarat goldfields and eventually bought Yallum Station, in south-east South Australia, for £30,000, in 1861. Realising that the narrow, approx. 17-mile (27 km) seam of rich red earth, the *terra rossa*, and the cool climate were ideal for grape-growing, he planted acres of vines which flourished.

Today, the 13,600 acres of vineyards stretch from Bordertown in the north to Kalangadoo near the southern coast. His grandson, John Riddoch Rymill, was a distinguished polar explorer and his great-grandson, Peter Rymill, established the Rymill Coonawarra Winery in 1990.

Dotted along the main north–south road, the 16 wineries and 23 cellar-door outlets provide tempting stops to sample the wines. Cabernet Sauvignon vines make up half of the varieties grown, but Shiraz, Chardonnay, Malbec, Pinot Noir and Riesling are also popular. Expert vintners blend different varieties to produce some of the world's finest reds. We sat in front of roaring fires – July is the middle of winter and can be pretty cool – and sipped at deep red wines, crisp whites and even a few rosés.

When we lived there in the early 1970s, we were blasé and somewhat ignorant of the wine's finer points. We held 'bottling parties', where a group from the town purchased large 44-gallon drums of white and red wine, which we set up in a back garden. Empty wine bottles were scavenged and a corking machine borrowed. Then the bottling began. Of course we had to sample the quality, as well as sucking on the tubes to draw out the wines from the drums. It wasn't long before it was a very merry band. Unfortunately, we ran out of corks, but ever-resourceful, Bill nipped across to the chemistry lab in the high school where we taught, and *borrowed* the corks from there. Their previous use as corks for the jars of chemicals stored there didn't seem to harm the taste of the wine at all!

Thirty miles north of Penola lies one of Australia's World Heritage areas, the Australian Fossil Mammal Sites at Naracoorte. The same limestone which provides the drainage for the vines has been eroded here by groundwater to form vast underground caverns. The first of these caves to be discovered was Blanche Cave in 1849, and it immediately became a popular venue for concerts and balls, which has continued till the present day. The first Underground Music Festival was held here in 1995 under the auspices of the Arts Council of Australia.

Further caves were discovered and the whole area became a tourist Mecca, so much so that in 1885, it was put under Government control and a caretaker appointed. By 1900, eight caves were open to the public and in 1908, the caretaker, William Redden, discovered Alexandra Cave. This cave has a magnificent collection of naturally formed stalactites, stalagmites and other spectacular decorations.

But it was Victoria Cave, discovered in 1894, which was to lead to the area's designation as a World Heritage Site.

In 1969, a young palaeontologist, Dr Rod Wells, and his team broke through into a new section of the cave in which lay the remains of tens of thousands of fossil vertebrates. He described how he felt when he crawled into the cave space at Naracoorte and saw the mass of bones lying there. His heart rate increased as he realised what he had found. It was as if he was a modern-day Howard Carter opening Tutankhamen's tomb. Excavating the cave and classifying the finds has been his life's work ever since.

When we visited the site in the early 1970s, the excavation had only just started and all that visitors could see was a small opening with a few bones scattered about. Rumours abounded about the strange creatures found there, but nobody knew for sure.

Now when we revisited the caves and discovered the Wonambi Fossil Centre, we realised just how extraordinary the creatures were. Almost 100 species have been found, dating back 300,000 years, with one-third of them now extinct, one-third living in other Australian areas, and the final third still found locally. Some of the extinct creatures have been painstakingly recreated by model-makers from the research carried out in the caves. Many of the fossils found are of megafauna; giant kangaroos (*Procoptodon goliah*) almost 3 metres (9 feet) tall; a constricting snake (*Wonambi naracoortensis*) up to 6 metres (20 feet) long; a giant wombat, the largest marsupial to ever live (*Diprotodon optatum)* that weighed almost 3 tonnes; and a 6-metre-long (20 feet) monitor lizard (*Megalania prisca*). Other creatures have no modern-day equivalents; a marsupial lion (*Thylacoleo carniflex*); and a hippopotamus-like creature (*Zygomaturus trilobus*), which shovelled up clumps of grasses with its front incisors.

Today, other fossil sites have been found, particularly in north-west Queensland, as well as in Burra, north of Adelaide, South Australia.

When we met up with Professor Wells in 2009, at another fossil site he was excavating north of Burra, he told us that one of his research students had been looking into Aboriginal dreamtime stories and finding links between them and the fossil creatures. Descriptions of encounters with megafauna in the tales have been corroborated by the fossil finds at Naracoorte and elsewhere.

We camped at Naracoorte that night too full of magnificent wines and wholesome pub food to move, and dreamt of giant kangaroos and marsupial lions roaming the red earth.

– 11 –

NEW FAMILY

Bill had always assumed he was an only child, with only a few family members that his parents kept in touch with. But in fact, he had large families on both sides that he knew nothing about. His father came from a large number of children from the two marriages of his mother, but he was a quirky character, quick to take offence, so Bill had very little contact with any of them.

When we took jobs in Canada, we were allocated places on the *Empress of England*, and sailed to Montreal from Liverpool. We didn't enjoy the journey much. We're not good sailors, and after the first night when the ship had headed into open seas, we woke to nausea and dizziness and the need for a sick bucket. Even going up on deck didn't improve our seasickness, but at least we could heave over the side, along with several other passengers.

But once we reached the calm waters of the St. Lawrence River, we recovered just in time to disembark. The night before, we had queued to receive our immigration papers to save time in Montreal. Bill studied his, a puzzled look crossing his face.

'These aren't my papers,' he said, 'but whoever they belong

to, they must be related to me.' Sure enough the surname was the same but the first name was 'Francis', and the place of birth was the same as Bill's – a small village in Lanarkshire.

We hatched a plan to find this guy among the hundreds of passengers. When we disembarked, our hold luggage was organised along the quay in alphabetical order. While Bill organised a porter, I stood next to ours and of course the mysterious Francis's luggage was right beside it. Sure enough, he turned up with his wife and claimed his luggage. And I claimed to be his cousin's wife! Yes, indeed! His dad was one of Bill's dad's brothers, but they hadn't spoken to each other in years. Francis, or 'Frank' as he was known, and his wife were teachers too, travelling to Canada for a better life and to see the world. They were heading north of Toronto to a small rural school, but we exchanged addresses and have kept in touch ever since.

But the biggest surprise was in 2015. Dave, the partner of Margaret, one of Bill's second cousins, was keen on genealogy and had built up a huge family tree by researching various documents and registers held online. He had posted this document on a popular website devoted to those with such an interest, then sat back and waited. Sure enough, someone contacted him. He replied and checked on this person to ascertain if she was who she said she was.

One Sunday afternoon, Dave emailed us to tell us the news. This person lived in Australia and claimed that Bill's mother was her granny. After checking for dates and family knowledge, the lady indeed turned out to be Bill's niece. Addresses and phone numbers were exchanged and later that day I found myself talking to Mary, one of Bill's new Australian nieces.

Bill, as usual, had gone out for a run and arrived back sweaty and puffed, to converse with his new relation. Her dad was Bill's half-brother, who was 12 years older than Bill and living in Sydney, Australia. And there were around 40 new family members for Bill to get to know.

By the end of the week, we had met up. Mary was in Scotland visiting her two sisters who lived here and they all came to see us. Gradually we built up the story around Bill's mum.

She had become pregnant – what happened to the father or even who he was, we don't know – and had given birth to a son, Neil. As an unmarried mother in the 1930s, she could have given him up for adoption, but she wanted to keep him, so he was brought up by her parents while she began her training as a mental-health nurse, in order to earn enough to look after him.

She met Bill's dad, Willie, in the hospital she worked in. He was also a mental-health nurse, who had given up working down the local pit for what he considered to be a safer and cleaner job. They married during the Second World War and she had another son – Bill. But Neil's connection to the family was kept very quiet. Bill remembers him coming around and, in fact, Bill's dad taught him to drive. As Neil was 12 years older than Bill, it meant that the age gap limited contact between them. Neil had married and had two children before he decided to emigrate to Australia as a '£10 Pom' in the 1950s.

I can only imagine how his mum had felt when we announced we were off to Canada in 1969. Both her sons had left Scotland to live abroad. After that searing farewell at Central Station in Glasgow, we never saw her again. She died suddenly, six months after we left.

Neil, however, stayed in Australia, moving around the country as work took him. He spent a lot of time with his family in the far north of the country, the Kimberley, where work was easier to come by and well paid, and it suited him. By this time, his family had grown to eight children, who moved with him, changing schools regularly. At one point they moved to New Zealand where some of the family still live.

Later we discovered that the family had been living in South Australia at the same time we were there. If only we had made contact with them then!

After the momentous news about Bill's long-lost and newly discovered family, there was nothing for it but to plan a trip out to Australia to meet up with Mary and the rest of the family in Western Australia.

We planned to go in July, starting in Perth, taking a guided tour across the Top End from Broome to Darwin, before heading to Sydney to meet up with Neil and his second wife, Edna. Mary, however, had a surprise for us. She had persuaded her dad, Neil, to make the trip to Scotland to see Bill and his old haunts. I wasn't to tell Bill, it was to be a surprise. One of Mary's sisters, Karen, who lived in a beautiful house near Dollar, had organised a family get-together to which we were invited, along with our son, Ronan, and his wife, Julie. Christopher was working in London at that point.

So one spring morning just as we were getting ready to drive to Dollar, Mary phoned to say that her dad was very emotional about meeting with Bill and perhaps it wasn't a good idea to keep it a surprise in case it was too much for Bill as well. So I told him and gave away the surprise which was probably just as well. I was amazed to see that he took it quite calmly

In the event it was a very emotional meeting indeed. They sat together on the sofa and shared memories and news about their lives.

In 2016, we made a long trip to Australia, starting in Perth, Western Australia, meeting up with Mary and most of the family there. Then after crossing the Top End, Broome to Darwin, we flew to Sydney to meet up with Neil at his home.

Neil died in 2023, aged 91, leaving behind his wife and another son.

– 12 –

BLOGGING: AUSTRALIA, JULY 2016

I wrote a series of blogs after our Australia trip in 2016 across the Top End, which I posted on my website (annburnett.co.uk), and have included a few of them here with some added extra bits.

Kimberley trip: Meeting up with our fellow travellers

It's 5 a.m. on a chilly winter's morning in July. It's still dark and we're sitting in a hotel's open-air restaurant trying to stuff as much breakfast into us before we set off. We don't know how long it will be before we get a chance to eat again. Other couples huddle around us exchanging wan smiles as they wander around the buffet for cereal, toast, tea and coffee. The poor girl rostered to serve us at this early hour looks as if she can't wait to get rid of us so she can return to bed.

We're all wearing shorts, warm jackets and stout walking shoes. Beside us lie various backpacks laden with water bottles, sunscreen, hats and cameras. Our luggage has already been portered to our transport, a converted 4-wheel-drive flatbed truck with a seating pod containing 20 seats. We will become only too familiar with this vehicle over the next 16 days.

We're in Broome, right at the top left-hand corner of Western Australia, and we're about to start an epic trip along the unpaved Gibb River Road into the Northern Territory, ending in Darwin. It's only open over the dry season, April to October, as during the wet months the road is flooded and impassable.

We met our guide and some of our fellow travellers yesterday in the hotel lobby. Gary, our guide, is in his thirties, from Belfast, we discover the moment he speaks, and he has fallen in love with 'the Kimberley' as this area is known. His enthusiasm is infectious, his manner open and friendly and within a couple of days he has us all whipped into shape and following his instructions to the letter.

I was worried that this trip would challenge me in many ways. Would I be fit enough to do the many walks scheduled into the itinerary? Would we be the oldest in the group, not exactly being spring chickens? Would there be many other foreign tourists? Would we fit in okay? Would we?

The meeting in the hotel reassures me on many fronts. For a start the rest of the party are all Australians and some look quite a bit older than us, though age is no indicator of level of fitness as we will find out. But it doesn't take long for us all to chat away, the Aussie sense of humour coming quickly to the fore, and confidences regarding various ailments exchanged.

By 6 a.m., we're all on board the bus and setting off. We've bagged the front seat but not for long, as Gary explains the movable feast that covers the seating arrangements. Basically, we move back a seat every day until we reach the back seats set over the axles, which make for an even more bumpy ride, at which point we are promoted to the front and the sequence starts again.

He gives us a quick tour of Broome as the sky lightens and, as we reach the white sands of the long Cable Beach, deserted at this hour, we park and watch the sunrise over the ocean. Yes, it's the Pacific Ocean and this is Western Australia, but the land has curved back on itself so that we are facing east.

At first we're driving on bitumen, but it's not long before we hit the unpaved road and the corrugations. Several hours of this and we're grateful to stop and stretch our legs at Windjana. We walk along the river, Gary pointing out the freshwater crocodiles on the opposite bank. The 'freshies' are smaller with narrower snouts than the big saltwater ones, the 'salties', and are not nearly as dangerous.

'They won't kill you. Their snouts can't get a good grip of you,' he reassures us, 'though they can still bite you quite hard.'

We squat on the sandy beach for lunch, the freshies far enough downstream to pose no threat, and then we're back on the bus and off to Tunnel Creek. This is a walk, or rather a paddle, through a natural formed tunnel through the Napier Range, which opens out into an idyllic watering hole at the end. I'm glad of the walking pole I borrow from the bus's supply to keep my balance in the stony, shingly waters.

By the time we reach our final destination, Bell Gorge Wilderness Lodge, it's dark and we're tired, cold and hungry. We're sleeping in posh tents, perched on a wooden base and large enough to hold a bedroom and bathroom, complete with shower and flush toilet. A hot shower, a three-course meal and we tumble into bed exhausted at 8 p.m. It's been a long day!

Kimberley: Next day

So where are we? We're in the Kimberley, one of the last wildernesses in the world and one of the least populated areas anywhere. It's right at the north end of Western Australia and its eastern edge is the border with the Northern Territory.

The Gibb River Road on which we're *rickety-rickety* travelling is unpaved, though the graders go through it regularly in order to smooth out the worst of the corrugations. The route is only open from around March to October, depending on the rains, which are heaviest in their summer months (November to February), and which regularly flood the roads and the settlements. Some of the roadhouses mark each year's flood or post pictures of how high the waters came. And when it's too bad to drive, the road is closed to all traffic.

There is another road, a bitumen road further south, the Great Northern Highway, for those who don't have 4-wheel drive vehicles, but hey, where's the fun in that? So we *rickety-rickety* our way, thankful to be strapped in as we bounce along.

It's beautiful country with creeks and rivers flowing all year round, home to huge numbers of birds. Rugged red sandstone cliffs give way to oases of waterholes surrounded by gum trees and grasses, their images reflected in the still waters. Waterfalls tumble down the cliff sides, and as the sun sets, the colours change to misty blues and greens and golds.

Darkness falls around 5.30 p.m. here in July and the temperature plummets. We pile on layers of clothing and huddle round the campfire before dashing off to our beds in the hope of retaining some of its warmth.

The nights are punctuated by rustlings and snortings under

the floorboards of the tent, or by the gentle and not-so-gentle snores of our neighbours. We coorie under the bedclothes and refuse to let our imaginations go to work on what those noises could be.

We're woken each day between 4 a.m. and 5 a.m. by the dawn chorus – a chattering and warbling and downright squawking that doesn't happen in Scotland. The only bird I can recognise is the kookaburra with its chortling sound. We do have a small alarm clock but we're always awake before it buzzes. Others are stirring in the adjacent tents so unwillingly, we creep out of our beds and dress. One morning, it's so cold (it sank to 5°C/41°F that night) that I slip my clothes into the warm bed with me and get dressed in a horizontal position. I used to do that when I was growing up in a tenement in Glasgow, but I was a great deal more agile then as my heavy breathing and contortions reveal.

Meals are in open-sided pavilions and are amazingly good considering the isolation of it all. It's not as if you can nip down to the shops if you've forgotten anything. Breakfasts are hearty, with a variety of choices that many a hotel would find hard to match. There's only one problem; there's only 45 minutes between arriving for breakfast and leaving on the bus, scarcely enough time to fill your stomach, gather your belongings and head for your seat. No one wants to be last on the bus!

Bill finds this well-nigh impossible. He's used to a leisurely breakfast followed by equally leisurely ablutions and a read of the morning paper. This dawn-rushing is not to his taste. We try arriving early for breakfast but they're not ready, so we still have to wait, wrapped in the alpaca-wool ponchos which are supplied to keep us warm in the early morning chill.

What to wear is another difficulty. The temperature may be in single figures before dawn, but after the sun rises, it heats up and may reach 30° Celsius (86°F) in the afternoon. So layers are the answer. They can be divested and stuffed into our backpacks as the day progresses. But we have another problem. The size and weight of our luggage (16 kg/35 lbs) is strictly limited, due to space on the bus being at a premium. That's okay if you're only doing the two-week trip before returning home, but we have an extra three weeks to cater for. And we have a variety of scenarios to dress for: cities, fancy restaurants, long walks through the wilderness, family get-togethers and swimming in waterholes, and temperatures ranging from downright cold to 45° Celsius (113°F). 'Coordinated layers' might be the term for it, but by the end of the holiday I am heartily sick of wearing the same things in whatever combination I can think up.

I forgot/couldn't pack a decent pair of shoes so I have: a. hiking shoes; b. Velcro-fastening sandals; and c. a free pair of flip-flops from M&S – they call them 'thongs' here (snigger, snigger). Work that lot into the equation.

But among all this stunning scenery, who cares what I look like?

Dunnies

At our age, (in our early seventies) toilet facilities are important, so we were pleased to read in the booklet we got about our trip that each of our overnight stops had en-suite facilities. Most impressive in the middle of nowhere! But more of them later.

En route along the unpaved road, things were different. There was no shortage of bushes, trees and scrub to crouch behind, after first of all ascertaining that there were no nasty creatures lurking nearby. By the end of the trip we'd all got quite used to men in one direction, ladies in the other and a communal mooning at anybody unfortunate enough to be passing.

It was the dunnies that were ... *interesting*. (An Australian toilet is a 'dunny', by the way.) To have any sort of toilet in a wilderness area is a feat of logistics, and many and varied were the solutions to the problem of where to put it and how to dispose of it. Some dunnies were of the simple 'long-drop' variety – a ramshackle shed with a *long drop* into some sort of pit, where it would eventually compost. The flies loved these. And the smell could be pretty overpowering too. But they gave you privacy and they always had toilet paper!

Others were more sophisticated, with buckets of some kind of disinfectant and instructions on washing down the toilet bowl after use. They also usually had a trapdoor in the bowl which kept the flies and smell out, and which opened when a lever was hauled back and forth. Noisy, but effective.

Our bus was loaded with a water tank, liquid soap and anti-bacterial handwash so we managed to avoid any episodes of the runs – or at least, no one admitted to them.

In the roadhouses we stopped at, most had flush toilets – Oh, the luxury! But they came with warnings. 'Put the lid down to keep out frogs and snakes,' they admonished. Apparently creatures come through the septic tank system and up the toilet bowl.

Gary, our guide, told us a tale of a young girl in her early twenties who had been bitten by a snake when she sat down on the toilet, and was so embarrassed by where the bite was that she told no one. Two hours later, she collapsed – it was probably a brown snake, one of the most venomous – and unfortunately, they couldn't save her.

It was certainly one way of making sure we put the lid down!

One night in our glamping tent, we discovered a frog sitting happily on the cistern in the en suite. It point-blank refused to return down the way it had come, so Bill simply closed the door of the en suite so that it would not come into the bedroom area. Another of Gary's tales was that frogs liked to seek out the warmest places to sit, and therefore they headed for your face in bed at night. Neither of us was happy with the thought of that frog, pretty though it was, spending the night with us.

I had been trying to ensure I didn't become dehydrated that day due to the temperature creeping up to around 38° Celsius (100° Fahrenheit) and had been regularly emptying my water bottle – they recommended we drink around 4 litres (7 pints) each day – so of course, the inevitable happened. In the middle of the night, I had to go.

Stepping gingerly on to the cold floorboards, I reached for my solar-powered torch. It was dead. I stretched my arms out to find the light switch. It wasn't where I thought it should be. I stepped forward and collided with the door of the en suite. I couldn't find the handle to open it. By the time I did manage to fling it open, things were desperate and I couldn't have cared if I'd stepped on the frog or even sat on it. Much relieved, I returned to my bed.

The next morning, the frog was clinging to the toilet brush, none the worse for its interrupted night.

Bumps and Bruises

Not everything on the trip went as planned. We crossed many creeks, some barely wet, others with fast-flowing water. One was very muddy. And stuck in the middle was a battered and well-used 4-wheel drive vehicle. The driver was standing by the roadside waiting patiently for someone to come along to pull him out. And that someone was us.

In no time at all, ropes were attached, our bus was put into reverse and gradually the 4-wheel drive was dragged back on to firm ground. Then another problem showed up. The vehicle wouldn't start. As the driver was the manager of the property where we were spending the night, it was deemed politic to stay and help. Anyway, the code of the outback is to do just that. Never ever leave someone stranded in the outback! It can be fatal.

They tried jump leads, but to no avail. Many were the suggestions offered by the males of our party, but nothing worked. In the end, the driver joined us on the bus and we took him with us to our lodgings where he commandeered a new alternator and a mechanic and they drove back to get his vehicle going again.

On another day, we were bowling along, or rather *rickety-ricketing* along, when the tread came off one of the front tyres. Fortunately, Gary had a spare so with all the men 'helping', it was changed in no time and we were on our way again. Half an hour later, the other front tyre lost its tread too, and this time we didn't have a spare. Gary had to use the emergency satellite phone to contact the nearest property which had a tyre and we all sat down to wait. What to do when stuck in the middle of nowhere? Make a brew! Tea and biscuits helped pass the time and we watched the sun set over the horizon just as the cavalry, in the shape of two guys in a ute arrived with the tyre. A 'ute' is an Australian truck with a flatbed at the back, useful for carrying, for example, sheep, extra cattle feed and plenty of booze (see chapter on Maureen and Barry).

We were very late to our lodgings at El Questro.

Bumps and bruises were not uncommon as we scrambled our way over rocks and stones on our walks into gorges or to Aboriginal art sites. The men in particular sported a variety of plasters over their cuts and scrapes. One guy tried an Aboriginal cure which consisted of spreading the red sap of a red bloodwood tree over his cuts. It looked pretty garish but he swore that they healed very quickly.

The worst incident was when Bill knocked himself out. He had been so busy watching where he was putting his feet as he scrambled along a path that he didn't notice an overhang and gave it what Gary described as a 'Glasgow kiss'. He was wearing his backpack which, as he fell backwards, prevented him from giving his head another knock. He appeared fine afterwards, though I was told to keep an eye on him. From watching various medical programmes I knew you were supposed to ask basic questions: Where were we? I didn't have a clue. What day was it? No, I wasn't sure of that either. Who was the prime minister? As we had left the UK just as David Cameron resigned, we hadn't heard who had taken over, being completely out of mobile-phone and internet range for days. And nobody was sure who the Australian prime minister was either, due to their complicated voting system.

Fortunately, Bill was fine, although if he had been badly hurt, the only option would have been to take him to the nearest airstrip and wait for the Flying Doctor to arrive. This is actually a charity which the people in far-flung areas of Australia rely on to help them when taken ill or hurt.

Helicopter Flight, Kimberley

We stayed at Mitchell Falls for a couple of nights in order to visit the waterfalls there. Helicopter flights were on offer, so we decided to go for it and booked a flight over the falls and out to the coast. The helicopter was small and a tight fit. Bill was fine – he was sitting up front with the pilot (who looked about 16 years old), but I was in the back with a guy, who would have made a marvellous rugby prop forward, and his wife.

Not only that, I was on the outside ... just about literally. The helicopter had no doors in the back (why bother with a door!) so I was perched on the edge of my seat feeling the breeze as we flew and looking straight down at the ground 35 metres (100 feet) below.

I loved it! I absolutely loved it!

It was exhilarating and exciting and I was safely strapped in, so there was nothing to fear as long as the engine kept going, the pilot didn't collapse and we didn't run out of fuel. Which of course it didn't.

The view over the falls was spectacular enough and must be truly wonderful in the wet season, but then we headed out to the coast over tracts of emptiness with very little evidence, if any, of man being there. The sea when we reached it was turquoise and deep blue, green in parts and every hue in between. There were numerous idyllic-looking sandy bays, but totally unsafe due to the crocodiles. We saw their tracks leading to and from the water, but of them, we didn't catch a glimpse. Not surprising as later on in the trip, in Kakadu, we realised just how well camouflaged they are on the riverbanks.

We followed the Mitchell River back from its mouth to the falls and beyond, and landed where our faithful bus was waiting to take us back to our Wilderness Lodge.

When we heard we could have another flight later in the trip over the Bungle Bungles, we were the first to sign up.

The Bungle Bungles are beehive-shaped dome structures made out of sandstone deposited about 350 million years ago and eroded over time by weather and water. Between them run deep chasms and gorges, some of which we walked into. They have striking orange and grey bands caused by bacteria (which make the black bands) or oxidised iron, which make the orange ones. As the sun lowers, the bands become even more distinctive.

Another young lad took us up in his helicopter with more space this time as there were only three of us, but still an absence of doors. However, this gives a much better view and it was well worthwhile. The southern end of the Bungle Bungles is where the domes are, but as you fly further north, there are fewer chasms and gorges and it becomes a high plateau. It was incredible to think that very few people indeed, if any, had ventured on to it and that it was as pristine a landscape as could be found anywhere in the world.

There were many strange and weird shapes left by erosion, which of course is still ongoing. The domes themselves are very fragile as they are only a thin skin of sandstone, which if pierced, reveals that they are filled with a grey sand. They are now part of

Purnululu National Park, which is also a World Heritage Site, owing to its natural beauty and outstanding geological features.

I'm glad we took the opportunity to fly as we saw so much more and got an overview of the areas which we didn't have on the ground. I can't wait till the next one!

East Alligator River

We crossed into the Northern Territory and headed for Katherine and Kakadu National Park. Water aplenty here and we enjoyed a variety of cruises down the Katherine River and especially the East Alligator River where crocodiles were much in evidence. After their numbers dropped to critical levels due to hunting and trapping, they became a protected species in 1971. Since then, they have made a remarkable recovery and are found everywhere in the Kimberley. We spotted many of them along the riverbank. They were hard to see at first, given their colouring and propensity to lie still, with only a bit of their snout showing above the water, but once we got our eye in and with our guide to help, we began to see just how prolific they were. Swimming in the many creeks and water holes now has to be done very carefully!

In the Darwin Museum we saw the stuffed carcass of the largest saltwater crocodile found locally. 'Sweetheart' was 17 feet (approx. 5 metres) long when captured in 1979, and died shortly after. A sad end to a magnificent creature.

Our guide on the boat sailing on the East Alligator River was Neville from a local tribe, skilled in the crafts of his ancestors. He demonstrated the art of making a paintbrush from the stem of a palm-like pandanus tree, which grows along the riverbank. He cut off a piece about the length he required, stripped off the outer layer, and with his fingers, pinged the fibres and they sprang into a brush shape. Instant paintbrush!

He also spoke of the need for the indigenous people to learn about both their own culture and that of the white settlers. He himself is a plumber to trade and when working in the Kakadu area with his two apprentices, one white, one Aboriginal like himself, the local indigenous people assumed that the white lad was the boss, despite being years younger than Neville.

We saw many examples of Aboriginal cave art on our travels through the area. Many have been dated back thousands of years and one site had a picture of a sailing ship and men wearing cocked hats. Was this evidence of early visitors from the Old World? We can't really be sure but there are reports of sailing ships long before Captain Cook, voyaging along the northern coast of Australia.

PART II

WANDERING AND WONDERING

– 13 –

THE LAST JOURNEY BEGINS, MARCH 2019

'I'm shocked,' Bill said and so he was. He looked it while I desperately held back my tears.

We were in the old hospital building that was waiting for demolition but still in use. Shabby, paint beginning to flake, everything in need of some TLC. But why bother when a mile away a brand-new, modern, flat-roofed facility was rising fast? In a few months it would be open, everything fresh, spanking new and this place would be left to quietly fade away until the council decided its fate.

Bill had driven there, parked badly, his wheel up on the kerb, before we went in to the waiting room. The place seemed almost deserted, only the occasional person coming out of one door and going in another. None were in a hospital uniform, all in mufti. We didn't have too long to wait before being taken in to the consultant's room. There was another older lady there as well, almost ready for retirement, though it was the consultant who retired not long after.

Pleasantries were exchanged and basic information – date of birth, full name, address, GP surgery – though I'm sure they had all that. Then Bill was taken away by the nurse for some testing while I was left to speak to the consultant. I couldn't for several minutes as I tried hard to control the tears and my shaky voice.

'I feel like I'm betraying him,' I eventually managed to get out.

I went on to relate what I'd noticed as a change in him: forgetting words; knocking into things; his inability to make up the IKEA bed we'd bought, while our son and I gave him the most basic instructions to follow; putting up a towel rail in the bathroom that took all day; being unable to read the bus timetable.

And there were problems with his driving. I was now the navigator-cum-instructor giving a running commentary on what and where was next. He could go through the physical motions of driving, changing gear and braking, but couldn't navigate. Nor was he very aware of other traffic, so I had to point out what was on his inside, or to watch out for a car coming up behind him. But as we were in a new part of the country, all roads were strange and different and we both had to be ultra-vigilant and aware.

My list went on and on until Bill and the nurse returned with the results of his tests. He'd been asked to count down from 100 in 7s: 100 – 7 = 93; 93 – 7 = ...

Then there was drawing a clock face and putting 3, 6, 9 and 12 on it.

Copying a square, following a pattern, remembering words and an address.

He scored in the 70s out of 100 in total.

People *without* dementia get the tests nearly all perfect. Anything less shows a lack of something, usually a degree of cognitive impairment – possibly dementia.

The consultant gave him just that diagnosis. 'I'm afraid you have dementia.'

No wonder Bill was shocked. 'I didn't expect that,' he said. 'I didn't think anything was wrong.' That, despite me crying and begging him to make a doctor's appointment. Despite me shouting at him for asking three times in ten minutes what time the food delivery was coming. Despite being aware that the bus timetable pinned to the bus stop was beyond his capabilities to understand.

We left with a prescription for a pill that would help, a handful of printed papers on dementia and links to local support agencies, and went home. I drove. He never drove our car again.

After his diagnosis of 'dementia, possibly Alzheimer's' I set about finding out everything I could about the disease and possible treatments, as well as what was available locally in the way of support.

There was a memory workshop in a nearby community, which was held in the local big house, now open to the public. There were several weekly sessions in which a variety of professionals told us about 'helpful aids', such as large-size clocks with easy-to-read numbers, devices to open jars and bottles, whiteboards to write up days and dates, phones with pictures of people to phone instead of numbers, stools to sit on in the kitchen and bathroom.

None of it applied to Bill ... yet. Nor did we want to know about it at that point. I had found a blog by a lady called Wendy Mitchell, who had been diagnosed with early onset dementia ten years earlier. As far as I was concerned, we had all that time ahead of us before we needed to consider such devices and aids. How wrong I was.

– 14 –

TESTS AND MORE TESTS

Bill agreed to do a driving assessment. He was convinced that he was perfectly able to drive and he would demonstrate that to the assessor. But the appointment was weeks ahead. Meantime he prepared for it by asking me to order a copy of the Highway Code, which he carefully read his way through. In addition, he covered pages and pages of A4 with his practice runs of taking away 7 from 100, drawing a clock face, following a pattern, and so on.

Bill's driving assessment was held in August 2019, at the Astley Ainslie Hospital in Edinburgh. Several buses took us near to the hospital, as I didn't know my way around the city with its bus lanes and complex one-way systems. They were also digging up roads for the new tram system, which made it worse. And anyway, the buses were impressive and free with our bus passes, so off we set. We hadn't realised that the hospital was on the far side of the grounds adjacent to Morningside Road, an area we'd got to know quite well when waiting for our new house to be ready, as we had lived in an Airbnb for several weeks and used to drive up there and park in Waitrose's rooftop car park.

So we had a long walk through the grounds till we got to the assessment centre. The lady was friendly and patient. But first, the dreaded paper tests: take 7 from 100; draw a clock face; follow a pattern; remember words. She even took him out into the corridor and made him walk up and down in a straight line. I knew that he wasn't going to pass. Eventually, she took him out in a dual-control car, round the hospital grounds first of all and then out and on to Morningside Road.

It's generally a busy road with traffic lights and pedestrian crossings and people nipping across the street to get to the M&S Food Hall, or into one of the many coffee shops. It's not the easiest road to drive along if you are not fully aware of your surroundings. I sat in the large waiting room, had a coffee and read all the notices pinned around the room. I couldn't tell you what they said. My mind wasn't paying attention – it was out on Morningside Road wondering how he was doing and if he would cope driving without me by his side giving a running commentary.

Through the window I saw them return after about 20 minutes. He was still in the driving seat and manoeuvred the car into a parking space. The lady was obviously talking to him. When they eventually came back into the waiting area, Bill behind her, he gave me the thumbs-down, his face registering the result even before he signalled it.

In her office, she went over why he'd failed. She'd had to apply her brake as he hadn't noticed the red light at the pedestrian crossing, as he was looking to turn right. So she'd stopped him before he mowed down the people crossing the road. There were other problems, less severe than that, but she was going to write to the DVLA and say that he was not fit to drive. If he surrendered his licence voluntarily, he could apply to get it back based on another assessment, if there was any improvement.

But I knew there wouldn't be. Dementia never improves. It's a one-way trip. There is no cure, just an inexorable creep along the infirmity of mind and body.

Bill was understandably upset. This was the biggest loss to him. Driving meant freedom, independence, not having to rely on me or public transport to go anywhere. He'd been driving long before he was eligible to have a licence, driving tractors on the hospital farm in the grounds of which his parents lived, driving his dad's car around the farm paths and grounds. But yet, when he'd come to sit his test, like most other exams in his life, he didn't do as well as expected and failed twice before finally getting his licence. He'd never had points, never had a speeding ticket – probably a case of pure luck as one of our sons was convinced the speed limit was 90 mph as he'd seen that on his dad's speedometer – and had driven in many different countries. He nearly got a ticket in Canada for having an overcrowded car when he took the entire school soccer team home from a game in his extremely large Plymouth Fury. The policeman phoned him later that evening to say he was cancelling the ticket, as he thought it was great that he was giving up his time to coach the youngsters.

We got the bus back into town and I took him to the Sheraton Hotel for something to eat. It was one of our favourite places when we felt flush and were celebrating Christmas or an anniversary. My appetite had returned and I was starving. All that emotion had left me with low blood sugar and a rumbling stomach. Bill fumed the whole time: it was unfair; it wasn't a proper assessment; he had noticed the crossing; the lady was biased; she'd made up her mind before she even took him out in the car. She probably had, given his scores on the paper tests and his inability to walk in a particularly straight line. I thought it was incredibly brave of her to take him out on to a busy road like that.

I chomped on haggis balls and listened half-heartedly. There was nothing really that I could say to help him. No pointing out how good the Edinburgh buses were, or how pleasant it was to take one into the city, how much petrol money we'd save. It struck me that any driving we needed to do would be up to me, not a prospect I fancied much. Having Bill drive for all those years had lessened my confidence.

He was annoyed for months afterwards, still hoping that he would improve enough to be able to get behind the wheel again. But I was relieved, as were our sons. Christopher had refused to get into the car if his dad was driving, preferring my elderly lady style, with a careful attention to speed limits and cautious approach to junctions.

We got a new car, an electric one, with no gear changes for me to struggle with. Our older son, Ronan, was an avid electric-car fan and talked us into it and it certainly was easier to drive and had far more power than the wee red VW up! that we'd had before. A charging point was installed outside the house as part of the deal and the salesman delivered the car to our door and took the petrol one away. Ronan came to show me the ropes of charging and driving it. It sounded like a spaceship as I switched it on and drove around the estate at 15 mph. Bill *humphed* and grumped and refused to take an interest as he wasn't going to be able to drive it.

From then on, I drove. It wasn't a pleasant experience driving him along to the supermarket as he made less-than-positive comments about my driving. Going past the high school when the kids came out was a nightmare. He would have me slow down to barely 10 mph which gave the pupils an opportunity to dive across in front of us, some even making rude gestures as they did so. More problematically, others would hesitate as we approached, not sure if we were stopping or not at the pedestrian crossing.

Parking at the supermarket was another flashpoint.

'Don't park next to anyone.'

'Get a quiet bit.'

'Not near any big cars. Keep well away from their doors.'

We usually ended up in the far side of the car park with a long walk to the entrance.

He used to do that too when we lived in Ayrshire. He'd always park far away from everyone else and get annoyed when others had parked beside him when we came out. But that was before he was diagnosed. Had dementia been creeping up on him even then?

– 15 –

LEWY BODY DEMENTIA

Dementia is a blanket term covering over 200 variants of the condition. The most common are Alzheimer's, Vascular, Fronto-temporal, Mixed dementia and Lewy Body dementia.

Lewy Body dementia (LBD) – also called Dementia of Lewy Bodies (DLB) – is the type that Bill was eventually diagnosed with. At first, he was given a CT scan and told that he had Alzheimer's with elements of Parkinson's. The consultant's report said: *the scan was unremarkable with no major abnormalities.*

Bill's sense of humour was still intact at that point, and he feigned disgust that his brain was classed as 'unremarkable'.

After Lockdown eased in late 2020, when I realised that he had deteriorated more than his fellow sufferers in our dementia group, particularly physically, I asked for a reassessment and after another CT scan the consultant diagnosed Lewy Body dementia.

Everybody with dementia has their own particular set of symptoms which makes it somewhat difficult to give an accurate diagnosis, but Bill's symptoms included difficulty in processing information. Standing at a bus stop one day, I realised he couldn't make head nor tail of the bus timetable posted up on the shelter. Another time I showed him a simple computer game matching three similar shapes, which he also had difficulty doing. I downloaded a set of games apparently appropriate for dementia sufferers, which included simple jigsaws of about 12 pieces, which again, he found difficult, and although he persevered at them for some time, they soon got put aside.

His muscles were affected: he lost many of his facial expressions, presenting instead a blank look. His voice faded. He had difficulty getting going when he wanted to walk. Eventually he couldn't sit up unaided, especially in the mornings, when his muscles wouldn't work at first. His bladder and bowel were also affected, necessitating catheters and pads. His swallowing ability came and went: at first it seemed like the main problem, but then it eased. Physiotherapy helped a lot. The patience and determination of the physio team at the local hospital to keep Bill moving worked until near the end. The last muscles to go were his legs. Years of running and various sports had made them strong and it wasn't until very near the end that they too, gave up.

He had hallucinations. He imagined he had done things which he hadn't, like being rude to people he met. He would go over events from long ago when he imagined he had committed social gaffes and the people concerned would no longer speak to him. Some nights, he had a cat in the bedroom or so he believed, or someone had got into bed with him. He thought he was back teaching, was always trying to find the headmaster's office and asking how long I'd worked there.

Anxiety is common in many types of dementia and he wanted me near him constantly, checking up where I was and calling for me in the night. He didn't like going anywhere new and the first day I took him to the day centre and handed him over to one of the helpers, he turned to me like a wee boy on his first day at school, anxious about me leaving him there.

He lost the ability to understand processes. This was a man with an honours degree in Physics and postgraduate diplomas in Educational Management, used to organising school–industry liaison days, skiing trips abroad, examination set-ups and school assemblies. Now he couldn't understand why he had to drink water and what it had to do with his catheter, and asked me repeatedly to explain it to him. Of course, dementia meant that he couldn't retain the information, hence I had to continually repeat it to him.

Like all dementias, there is no cure and eventually death is inevitable unless some other condition takes hold. The length of time people live with a dementia varies: some are still going after ten years, whereas others have a shorter life span. Bill managed almost exactly three years from diagnosis to death.

The drugs on offer we did not find very helpful. It was hard to tell if they were slowing down the whole process, and certainly Bill's disease galloped along with very little break or remission. He had pills to help with the hallucinations and anxiety, and pills to help him sleep longer and stop him waking in the early hours, which really was more of a help to me as I was suffering from exhaustion.

Physically his appearance changed as the weight dropped off him and his face got much thinner. I could feel his ribs when I hugged him and his skeleton became more obvious.

Other physical problems emerged. He had a hernia which needed repairing, but his dementia meant that clinicians were hesitant to operate as his breathing would be affected by the anaesthetic. Tests were carried out to see if his prostate was causing the retention of urine and he was given medication to shrink it. But no, the prostate was fine – it was the dementia that was the problem.

His skin became very dry, particularly on his face and head, and under his beard, which he'd let grow because of the difficulties he had with shaving. Various creams and oils were added to the bedtime routine in an attempt to lubricate the skin.

– 16 –

EMERGENCY CARE PLAN, MARCH 2020

I was advised by social workers to draw up an Emergency Care Plan so that if anything happened to me, or I wasn't able to care for Bill, they would know his routines and what he needed. This is one from the early days.

EMERGENCY CARE PLAN (MARCH 2020)

About Bill

Care and support required:

- Reassurance and confirmation of plans.
- Help with some aspects of care; e.g. choosing clothes.
- Help with medication: filling daily box, prescription ordering.
- Cooking meals apart from breakfast: helps himself to cereal etc.
- Fill hot-water bottle at night.
- Deal with issues from iPad and TV – changing channels, emails, etc.
- Explaining things and repeating as required.

Bill's routine:

- Up around 7–7.30 a.m., shave and shower.
- Long leisurely breakfast: cereal and dried fruit, then fruit, usually kiwi, followed by toast and jam or Danish pastry, tea. Reads news on iPad throughout breakfast.
- Unloads/loads dishwasher.
- Brush teeth, make bed and get ready for whatever we're doing. Doesn't like to be rushed. Panics slightly if have to be out early; e.g. hospital physio appointment on Wednesdays.
- Will go out for short run around 12 p.m. if weather okay, usually every 2nd or 3rd day. Takes an hour. Preparation time is lengthy.
- Late lunch or sometimes skipped. Biscuits and cheese, toasted cheese, cheese and pickles, cold meat and bread.
- Usually take it easy in afternoon. Coffee about 4 p.m. Deals with rubbish bins.
- Main meal around 6 p.m. – main course plus dessert. Empties /loads dishwasher. Watches TV in evening. Bed around 10 p.m.
- *Tuesdays:* singing group in Maitlandfield House Hotel at 12.30 p.m. followed by tea and chat till around 2.30 p.m. First Tuesday of month dementia-friendly meeting in hotel at 10.30 a.m.–12.00 p.m.
- *Wednesdays:* 10 a.m. appointment at Physio at new hospital, and at the moment followed by psychologist appointment at 11.30 a.m. Usually walks there and back himself.

Medications:

- 15g of memantine daily; i.e. one and a half pills, loaded into plastic pill box on table. Refilled on Saturdays.
- Eye drops to be used several times daily as required. In bathroom.

Food:

- Has difficulty chewing some meats unless slow-cooked till tender. Not keen on pork. Likes to snack on Nākd biscuits, nuts and raisins, chocolate.
- Dessert usually ice cream with fresh fruit if available.

Communication:

- Generally speech is fine though forgets words and names. Likes to correct himself without help.
- Writing and spelling giving some problems.

– 17 –

TRANSCRIPTS, MAY 2021

In my attempts to do as much as I could for Bill, I put my name down for Dementia Research, who were looking for people with lived experience of dementia to take part in various research projects. In March 2021, one of the researchers, a Ph.D. student, contacted me to say that she was looking for carers who were just in the process of having professional carers come in to help. I fitted the requirements exactly.

So for six months, from May to November 2021, I had a video call with Marianne for an hour every fortnight. I got a sitter in to look after Bill while I went upstairs and talked.

It was a lifesaver. To talk uninterrupted about my life and how I was trying to do my best to keep Bill at home allowed me to vent, rant, cry, and yes, to laugh for that one hour every fortnight.

The meetings were recorded and after the six months were up, Marianne sent me the transcribed conversations – over 100 pages. I had forgotten much of what happened during those months as things changed so quickly that I had little time to process all that was going on.

But they are a valuable record of our life at that time.

The following text is transcribed from the oral interviews between me and Marianne, the Ph.D. student, who was researching the effect of carers coming into the home.

18 May

AUTHOR: The only thing we have at the moment is six hours' respite care a week. So at the moment Zoe is the main carer who comes in, and she takes Bill out for a walk. And then when they come back, she'll give him his lunch and look after him for me, for three hours today and the same again on Friday. And that's it; that's all I've got at the moment. I'm kind of coping, but Bill's illness is progressing so quickly that from month to month things change and I don't think I've got long until I'm going to need more help. For example, a couple of nights ago I heard him coughing at one in the morning. I could hear him coughing and choking. This kind of dementia affects every single muscle in his body, including his throat, and he's been having trouble swallowing. The consultant did warn me that this was going to get worse. I got up when I heard him coughing and at one point I wanted the ambulance because he was having such difficulty, but I kept him sipping at drinks and eventually it cleared, but I think it's the way it's going to be going. That's the muscle group most affected but it's affected his face; he's got this very blank expression. It's affected his bladder and his bowels, his hands, everything – as well as the dementia in the brain.

MARIANNE: Quite a big physical element.

AUTHOR: He was diagnosed two years ago. Although I had been aware that things weren't quite right, I couldn't quite put my finger on it. I moved us over here from the west coast to be closer to our family and it was fine at first, but then I insisted he got to the doctor. In fact, I teed up the doctor first before he went along. She was ready for him and she gave him the works and sent him to the Memory Clinic. And it was there the psychiatrist picked up on dementia, just stated it was probably Alzheimer's. We just carried on.

We joined the local dementia group. We also joined a kind of subgroup, a singing group. That was good. Not that we could sing, but we were very fortunate in that one of the carers whose mum had it, was a music teacher and a brilliant singer and musician, so she led it and it was great fun. We were going to be on the local radio with a song we'd composed. Wonderful! And then Lockdown happened and when we came out of that first lockdown and started meeting again, not that we were allowed to sing, we'd meet outside in the grounds of the hotel. And it was then I became aware that Bill's disease was progressing far faster than any of the other dementia sufferers. So I went back to the doctor and we're very fortunate – he gave us his GP trainee who had plenty of time to spend with us, who was very keen to do as much as he could. So we were sent to every specialist you could think of and people were coming here: the occupational-therapy people, we had speech and language, we had the incontinence lot, we had everybody. And eventually he went for another scan and we saw this consultant geriatrician, who was extremely non-empathetic and rather blunt and said, 'Give him 18 months. Death could happen any time now because of this choking'. That was the end of November and that was awful, really awful.

So I decided then I'd better start the process of getting help. At first, Bill was adamant he didn't want help, he didn't want anyone in the house: 'We're fine, we'll cope.' But I couldn't. And then we had a lady who came. I got her privately. She came once just before the second lockdown just after Christmas, and the first thing she did was shake his hand and I thought, *No, we're not having that in a pandemic*. So I made the excuse that, as we were locked down again, we couldn't have anybody in.

But the ones I've got now … well, the carer today was saying how little training she's actually had, but she's a kind of ebullient type and that suits Bill fine. You know, she jildies [hurries] him on and puts his shoes on: 'Come on, out we go.' It gives me a wee break, but that's what we just have now.

* * *

MARIANNE: The next step is a wee bit less focused on the service and a wee bit hopefully more focused on you. What I would be interested to know is if you can describe how you see your role in your home. Or, who are you in your house? Who are *you*?

AUTHOR: I've changed. I have lost myself. I am now the carer. I've had to give up a lot of my own interests and activities and I found that hard. I feel my main responsibility is Bill and he needs everything I can offer.

MARIANNE: It's okay to get upset.

AUTHOR: I'm more upset these last months than I have been for years. I feel I've lost myself. At the same time, I feel I need to keep something of it going because I'm going to be on my own eventually – quite soon, probably – and I have to build my life again. So really I'm just the carer.

MARIANNE: Do you feel that you're able to keep yourself separate from being the carer, or do you feel like those things have merged together? Does that make sense?

AUTHOR: They are separate. When I wake up in the morning and I'm dreaming, I'm in the dream and suddenly I think, *Oh there's another life that's reality*, and it starts the minute I get up and I find it hard. I escape into books and some television if it's good ... though to go back to what I was saying ... I just haven't got the energy or an interest in going to [writerly things] because I can't devote enough time to it and I feel cut off from them all. I skim-read through all the wonderful things they're up to, which is rotten of me.

MARIANNE: I think that's okay. You have other things.

AUTHOR: I have to not indulge in all the things they're doing. Because I can't. I can't do it at the moment. Hopefully later on, I'll maybe get back to it, but things will have moved on by then and all my contacts and so on will have changed.

MARIANNE: Are there particular parts of the day that are more difficult than others?

AUTHOR: Yeah, I find when Bill displays how disabled he

is, I get upset, or if he says how depressed [he] is or mentally not with it, and when we're tired at night. Bedtimes are always difficult, sometimes one more than others.

I did speak to the social worker and say, 'Could I have somebody come in at bedtime? Maybe once or twice a week?' He said, 'You're either able to cope with putting him to bed or not, but it's got to be every night.' I thought, *You have never been a carer, have you? Because you know yourself some days it all goes smoothly and other days are a nightmare.*

He's been having the odd hallucination, usually at bedtime, when he's in bed. He's been complaining about a cat in the room or that somebody's got into bed with him, and it takes a while to get settled down after that.

MARIANNE: So the Social Work Department are saying you can either have support every night or not at all?

AUTHOR: Yes, whereas just a couple of nights a week would be lovely.

MARIANNE: Other parts of the day that you enjoy?

AUTHOR: First thing in the morning. If he is not immediately awake I can go down and have a cup of tea. I sit at a lovely window looking out over fields and trees and that's perfect. We have time together. Sometimes we watch a programme together and we quite enjoy it, or if we're meeting with friends, now that we're able to do that, that's good. Although [he's] really not able to join in very much because his speech is affected badly. There's things he wants to say but he's so slow everybody has to wait for him to get out what it is he wants to say, which must be so frustrating.

MARIANNE: So with the diagnosis of Alzheimer's … is that right or did they change his diagnosis?

AUTHOR: It was originally Alzheimer's but because of the changes, and the rapidity of it, they looked at it again, did more scans and decided it was Lewy Body dementia.

MARIANNE: So the next question is, is there anything, in particular in the last year, that was particularly significant for you? But as part of that, I'd also like to know how much you feel the whole situation with Lockdown has affected you.

AUTHOR: Lockdown hasn't been as bad as perhaps people think because nobody has been allowed to go out and I haven't been allowed to go either. The last few days, when people were saying, 'We're going out to this, we're going out to this and that, the theatres are opening and the historical sites are opening', I thought, *I can't go to them* … I'm envious of what they have because before I was quite happy because nobody was going anywhere and that suited me fine. It didn't make us stand out as being different. So although we missed seeing friends as much, we managed to wangle things, either with Zoom and so on, or meeting outside on walks and things. So we coped okay.

The main thing has been the geriatrician's comments about longevity. That really has upset us both. I mean at first, when he got the diagnosis of dementia, we looked around: someone had it for ten years, and you think, *Och well, we'll manage. Something else can take us away before then*. And then to have this diagnosis given – *prognosis*, I should say – was soul-destroying.

MARIANNE: Would you say that it was the prognosis that was the very difficult part, or the way in which it was given?

AUTHOR: The way in which it was given had a lot to do with it too. It was so unsympathetic, very blunt. I mean we had another session with a psychiatrist who gave us the results of the second scan, which confirmed Lewy Bodies. and her method of dealing with it was so much more sympathetic. So this is just his manner unfortunately.

* * *

MARIANNE: Can you describe how the future feels to you at the moment?

AUTHOR: I don't think too much. I wouldn't say I was totally prepared for it. I keep thinking about the funeral and what to do. I should bring it up with my sons, who are living in the area, but just haven't been able to. And thinking beyond.

We've been married all these years, so how will I do on my own? This is where, as I said, I've this network. I've got a lot of friends. At my age you get a lot of single widows, because they've all been through it and I'd look to them for support, but it's not something I'm looking forward to. But I have to look beyond it, because I don't know how long I'm going to live, but my mum was 94 and my father was 88. Unless I get hit by a bus or something, I've got good genes for the long run, but we'll see.

I mean, all this is inevitable, but I can't change it. We're just on this road and we have to go down it.

MARIANNE: Do you speak with Bill about the future?

AUTHOR: We have done a little when we got the diagnosis. He's not one for opening up. He was offered sessions with a psychologist early on, but when Covid started, it was put on to phone calls and he didn't like that at all, so he gave it up. But I think he found it difficult to open up, bit like most men. It's a very difficult subject to think about.

MARIANNE: Do you think that people find it difficult to ask you about it?

AUTHOR: Yes, they don't ask me about it. Even our sons are ... not in denial, but they don't want to talk about it either and I have to bring it up with them rather than do a sort of last-minute scramble to get things organised.

MARIANNE: Is there anything else you would like to talk about or tell me about? About your life with Bill?

AUTHOR: It just feels unfair that at this time of life, when we're both getting on, that we should be faced with the worst scenario that there could be, but that happens to everyone. I'm glad, when Bill retired, that we took off, did a lot more travelling than we'd done before, and had a great ten years of just spending our pensions. And we had a hell of a good time. We did some really interesting things. The first time, actually, I was aware of those problems was when we were crossing the Top End of Australia in 2016, on the dirt road, in a group. Our transport was a flatbed lorry with a kind of bus thing on top. Not exactly comfortable but interesting, and there was a group of us, some people even older than us, I have to say. The driver would take us so far and then he'd lead us in walks and things through the bush. And every morning we had to be on the bus for quarter to seven, breakfasted, dressed, packed and we had to pack a rucksack with what we needed for the day – water, suntan lotion, hats ... and that had all to be done. Now Bill couldn't do that. He'd stand there with the rucksack, then he put things in and took them out, put more in and took everything out and he panicked. It got worse and worse and I ended up doing it for him because we had to be on that bus. They were rotten, as the last person on the bus would get jeered, so nobody wanted to be last in the bus at quarter to seven in the morning. But that made me really think that things weren't right. His organisational skills were not up to scratch, and considering the amount of travelling we'd done in the past, that should have been automatic.

MARIANNE: But hard to put your finger on it at that point. Just thinking that that wasn't quite right?

AUTHOR: Yeah, because when you know somebody that well, it's the little things you notice that are different. He was absolutely shocked when he got the diagnosis. He could not believe it. He thought there was nothing wrong with him and he couldn't understand my nagging at him to go to the doctor, and it was quite fraught. And then when she said, 'You know, I think you've got Alzheimer's', he just stopped driving, That was it. I had to drive him home from the hospital. So he had a hard job coming to terms with it and he was totally unaware of his difficulties for a long time, whereas the rest of us were only too well aware of them.

When he put himself forward for a driving assessment, he was convinced he was going to pass, but I knew from his driving, he wouldn't. I mean the automatic, the mechanical way of driving, he could do – change the gear, signal and all this – but couldn't assess the traffic ahead of him and he had no idea of navigation. I was sitting beside him saying, 'You're going to turn right here, so move into the road now watch for this car'. It was as if I was driving and he was just going through the motions, but of course he failed it. The assessment is taken out on the roads and in a dual-control car and the assessor had to push down firmly and brake cos he'd missed a red light. He was really, really despondent whereas the rest of the family all breathed a sigh of relief that he wasn't driving any more.

MARIANNE: So, if Bill felt he didn't have a problem and the diagnosis was a shock to him, and failing the assessment was a shock to him, how did you feel about those steps that were happening? Are you saying that the family kind of felt some relief?

AUTHOR: Yeah we were all aware of it going on and I made it my business to make sure we were in touch with all the organisations and societies that had anything to do with dementia and could help us. And at first, I certainly felt, not relief, but okay about the fact that he has dementia, it lasts for a long time, until, of course, it became apparent that Bill's wasn't that type of dementia. Then the kind of bottom fell out of the world really.

* * *

AUTHOR: You asked who I thought I was now. I said just a carer and that's it. That's all I do, 24 hours a day. The first time I brought the carer in, I was free for a couple of hours. I went to Tesco and I couldn't believe the sense of relief. I felt so guilty, but at the same time I had been let out and I was free! I could browse my way around shelves. Now, shopping in Tesco is something I never enjoyed, but I find myself gloating over the baking aisle and all sorts of things and I thought, *how have I changed*?

MARIANNE: Do you think that's changed? I know you've only been getting that wee bit of time since January. Would you say that the way you use that time now has changed from maybe the first few times that you had the respite?

AUTHOR: I think it's beginning to. At first I think I was throwing myself into anything just for the change, not that I could do much due to Covid, but now we can meet friends, so I'm meeting a couple of ladies, one whose husband died of a similar thing to Bill's, and the lady whose parent has just gone into a home. So we've got plenty to talk about and share. And sometimes the black humour is very funny because of all we've had to do. Oh dear, I suppose it's like the police and doctors and things – the black humour gets you through.

MARIANNE: I think that's true. Sometimes, in times of darkness that's what people embrace. That can really help.

AUTHOR: I was just remembering this one Christmas, my

younger son was coming up from down south and then jokingly I said to him, 'Ah good, you could help wipe your dad's bottom', and he looked at me, horrified. Well, he could do that any time now. I never thought it'd come to that, but there you go.

MARIANNE: I think it's incredible how adaptable people can be.

AUTHOR: Yes.

MARIANNE: That's interesting actually. Have you surprised yourself?

AUTHOR: Many years ago when I was a student of Psychology like you, I took a summer job in a mental hospital down in the south of England. It was the geriatric ward, so not only were they senile but they had mental difficulties too, and the number of bottoms I wiped there was quite considerable.

MARIANNE: That sounds like probably an eye-opening experience.

AUTHOR: I loved it. I loved looking after them and caring for them. It was interesting from a psychological point of view with all the various illnesses there were and how it affected them. And also the physical conditions they had too, which had brought them into that ward. Now this is going back to the 1960s, so you know how in the Dark Ages Psychology was at that point. Some of the things that happened were not very nice. They were still using ECT [Electro Convulsive/Shock Therapy] and things like this.

MARIANNE: It's certainly different now, but I think that well into the 1980s and even still in the 1990s we would look now even and think, *Oh, that's how people are living in hospitals and things*. That's the end of my questions. But if you have any other questions or any other stories or thoughts then, I'm not in a rush.

AUTHOR: It's just nice to open up, because you can't do that with other friends who are not in the same position. I was speaking to a friend on the phone and I was laughingly saying, 'God, see trying to get trousers on!' And she said, 'Why are you putting his trousers on?' I said, 'Because he can't.' She had no idea. She hasn't seen him because of Covid and she doesn't realise the position I'm in, so there's no point in telling the likes of her about what life's like. But friends who've been through it all, you can share a wee bit, but you don't want to burden them with all this – the moans and the groans – but sometimes we do.

– 18 –

HELP AND SUPPORT

In 2019, after Bill was diagnosed, I discovered a dementia-friendly group which met every month in the local hotel. It was advertised as a friendly informal get-together with tea and coffee, which I thought sounded ideal. It met at 10 a.m. till around midday, so we thought we'd drop in about 11 a.m. or so. We walked into the meeting area to discover a crowd of people sitting round a table as if in a formal meeting, listening to a lady who was discussing various activities. It was nothing like the *informal* gathering I had envisaged.

However, the organiser greeted us by giving each of us a hug and arranged extra chairs to squeeze around the table. Someone else got us a cup of coffee and a biscuit and we settled down to hear what was being said.

It was a mixed bag of people. Some were obviously suffering the effects of dementia, but the majority looked 'normal', I thought, being unable to distinguish between *carers* and the *cared for*. They were planning various outings and trips, including one to Stornoway to meet up with a gentleman there who was writing and producing film and theatre shows on the subject of his dementia, and to view his latest production. Of course we signed up for it. We hadn't travelled much since our trip to Australia in 2016 and we felt we'd like to see a bit of Scotland as well. I had been in Stornoway when I was a student, to visit a friend, but had been horribly seasick on the crossing. This time we would be flying.

I don't know what happened. Apparently there were too many of us wanting to go and funding wouldn't stretch that far. So the trip never happened.

However we did have an outing to the Kelpies and the Falkirk Wheel, with a boat trip on the Wheel and along the canal, followed by afternoon tea at Callendar House, a former teacher-training college. It was a beautiful day and we sat out in the sun at the Kelpies with coffees, and met up with Anne and her mum, who had been diagnosed with Alzheimer's. Anne was to become an important friend and support in our lives.

Later that summer, Anne asked if we would go with her and her mum to a meeting where Music in Dementia was the topic. It was in a community centre in one of the coastal towns and as usual we were late. We couldn't find it and I couldn't get parked close by. Bill was never one for leaving on time to get anywhere – getting to his work in a school was always a mad dash out of the door at the last minute, even although he'd been up for hours. And now that I was having to do all the driving, I always liked to add an extra ten minutes of 'getting lost' time. I still do.

So of course we were running late and I got lost, which made us later. But we were welcomed and joined the group, who were sitting in a circle. Everyone had to introduce themselves and say what they did in the creative industries. It was quite a high-powered group. One of them demonstrated her prowess by bursting into song – a rather awkward moment. The organiser ran a group in another of the coastal towns, and others represented support groups, community music groups, and the like. I said that I had just become a carer for Bill, whereas he surprised me and everyone else by announcing with great aplomb that he was 'one of the grateful recipients of your input'. I suspect that his tongue was firmly in his cheek.

The workshop organiser explained how she ran her group, and burst into song at regular intervals. I don't know if we were expected to join in, but nobody did. She was obviously very enthusiastic about singing in the folk-music tradition. However, later Anne and I agreed that it wasn't the route we wanted to follow.

From that meeting, Anne decided that she would start up a local wee singing group for those with dementia and their carers. She is a talented musician and teacher, and steers many pupils towards scholarships and university placements, as well as instilling a love of music in children from babyhood up. The singing group started out as an offshoot of the monthly dementia meetings, when those interested would hive off at the end of the meeting for a brief singing session. Bill wasn't keen, not being a singer. Not that I was either, but because it was Anne, who had quickly become a friend, we joined in. Originally there was Anne and her mum, me and Bill, Pat and John, Linda and her mum Jane, Margaret from Prestonpans, and Mike and Gloria.

It grew into a weekly get-together in the hotel with a regular group attending. An hour's singing followed by an hour's chat and coffee. At our sessions, Anne played an electronic piano which she'd bought with funding from the local high school, and took us through a repertoire of songs she thought would appeal to us.

Lots of traditional Scots ones at first – 'Westering Home', 'Dumbarton Rock', 'The Black Island', 'I Love a Lassie' – none of which appealed to Bill and his more eclectic tastes of The Chemical Brothers, Rod Stewart and The Rolling Stones. But the company was good and afterwards we went for coffee in the hotel lounge. There we exchanged news and experiences and learned much about dementia and the help available. This included: Attendance Allowance and how to fill in the forms; Council tax help; and Blue Badges for the disabled, not that they couldn't walk far, but because they were a danger to themselves and others in car parks, as they could step out into traffic.

Even more important was the support and shared experiences of those who had been through it all and come out the other end still with a life. Marjorie, who'd lost her husband to dementia the previous year, had joined and was a reassuring and friendly presence. If I described any of Bill's symptoms, she could assure me that George, her husband, had felt/done the same and would then tell me how she had coped with it ... or not.

Covid Lockdown in early 2020 stopped it all. We were forced to meet up on doorsteps when out for the daily walk that we were allowed. Eventually, as restrictions eased slightly during the summer, we were able to meet as a group, but outside and with no singing.

So we did so in the spacious hotel gardens. Firm friendships were formed and information and advice on dementia issues were exchanged. We learned a lot about the disease and its progress from seeing our friends so frequently. And it was from that, that I realised that Bill's illness was progressing far quicker than the others in the group.

What struck me was how far Bill had deteriorated in the

weeks since we had last met up. At first when we joined the group, Bill was one of the less-disabled members, but now, the difference in him was marked. He was now one of the most affected by dementia, particularly physically. He was losing his muscle power. I was concerned enough to go back to the doctor and ask for further investigations.

Gradually, Bill became more and more upset at the group. He couldn't sit comfortably because of all the weight he was losing. Marjorie used to bring him a folding camping chair, while I supplied the cushions to enable him to sit comfortably in the hotel gardens. But he couldn't get comfortable on the chairs inside. Also the carpet was patterned and in his eyes, it moved and made him nauseous. We would get up and I would walk him around the room for a bit. It was only later I learned that this was a common symptom of many forms of dementia.

I was also upset. The words of the songs we were singing now struck home and I would find myself in tears while trying to sing 'Some Enchanted Evening', 'Ae Fond Kiss', 'Leaving on a Jet Plane', 'What a Wonderful World'.

Eventually Bill decided to stop going to the group and I got a sitter in to stay with him while I went. It was my only outing of the week where I could meet up with supportive friends.

I have a video I took of Bill and his great pal John walking round the lawn at the hotel using their walkers. Competitive to the end, they're having a race and John, though a good ten years older, is pulling ahead of Bill, concentration etched on their faces. John is dead now too, although he lasted six months longer than Bill.

But the singing group goes on with new members and carers, and I and the other widows of past members still attend, deriving solace, comfort and a hell of a good laugh from the group. Perhaps a few tears are let slip at some of the lyrics we sing, but nobody minds and everyone understands. And it's part of our remembering.

– 19 –

THERAPIES

Physiotherapy

Towards the end of 2019, Bill attended a physiotherapy class in the new hospital. It was quite a change from the old hospital, where he had been diagnosed. Here was a new gym with brand-new equipment and qualified physiotherapists, who worked with him to keep up his levels of fitness and hopefully keep him running.

Every Tuesday morning he would set off to walk to the new hospital for the 10 a.m. class. I helped him to leave around 9.45 a.m. in order for him to get there on time. I packed his rucksack for him, with a bottle of water, and sometimes suitable shoes if the weather was poor and he arrived with wet and muddy walking shoes. I remember having to do the same in 2016, when we'd been on the trip across the top of Australia and I'd pack his rucksack every morning.

Bill enjoyed the class and the exercises they gave him. His physio encouraged him and monitored his progress. Bill felt positive about the class and his abilities to still keep running. Then Covid struck and everything shut down. The class stopped. The physio Lawrie was excellent and phoned Bill every two weeks to see how he was doing and to keep up his morale. I would answer the phone and while waiting for Bill to make his way to it, I would chat with him. I discovered that we were both keen gardeners and each time, we compared the progress of our vegetable patches.

By the time Lockdown was lifted and the class could begin again, Bill had deteriorated considerably and wasn't suitable for the class. He was devastated. I managed to get him reconsidered, but this time for an individual session. Lawrie and his boss came out to the house to check Bill over and to see what they could offer him.

Lawrie wasn't what I'd expected. From our chats on the phone about gardening, I had envisaged a man somewhere in middle-age, but here on my doorstep was a young man with spiky hair, tattoos and piercings and a great deal of enthusiasm to do his best to help Bill. They decided that he could attend an individual session once a week. He was no longer able to walk up to the hospital so I took him there instead and joined the wife of another client for a coffee in the café while our husbands were put through their paces.

Bill managed to attend the session until the end of December 2021, when the sessions ended. But then he was taken to hospital at the beginning of February 2022, no longer able to stand and approaching the end. I'm sure that Lawrie and his team were instrumental in helping him stay at home for as long as he did.

Speech and Language Therapy

Another specialist who came to visit was the Speech and Language therapist. Bill's voice had faded and he was finding it difficult to project his voice so that we could hear him. Forgetting his words was one thing, but being unable to speak up made it worse. She showed him exercises, including shouting at the wall, which certainly helped to develop his voice.

Unfortunately, there were many other exercises and methods for the many symptoms of his disease which he was also required to carry out, so perhaps developing his voice didn't get as much attention as it should have.

Dietary Advice

The dietician came too. Swallowing proved problematic and she wanted to ensure that his diet was giving him as much nutrition as possible, in as easy a way for him. Hard-to-chew foods like meats were out, though he could still manage a plate of mince or some spaghetti bolognese. He was able to handle soft foods like eggs and pasta, but a bacon roll was too much, which was a shame because he loved that. Even chopped up small, bacon just wouldn't go down safely. His favourite food was ice cream, especially salted-caramel flavour, so every night he got a plateful. Sometimes he refused the main course, it not being to his liking, and instead would wolf down a bowl of ice cream.

Breakfast was usually a bowl of bran flakes with banana and milk, though the dietician suggested fruit juice rather than milk, to see if that would help with the excess saliva he was producing – yet another problem to contend with.

Then he would have a cup of tea with a straw to save him having to lift up the cup, and a Danish pastry cut up into little pieces.

He became an incredibly slow eater, his food cooling far more rapidly than he could eat. So despite trying plate warmers, his food had to be reheated in the microwave.

When he was in hospital, they provided him with puréed meals. I used to go in to see him at lunchtime so that I could feed him and help the nurses, who had several other patients to feed as well. I was always surprised by what was on the menu for him. Sticky toffee pudding was his absolute favourite.

The weight fell off him. He'd always been slightly built and when he was running, he liked to keep his weight quite low. But before I suspected there was anything wrong, he set about losing as much weight as he could, much to the concern of family and friends, as he began to look quite gaunt. He thought he would be able to run faster carrying less weight, but I wonder if this was one of the signs of dementia that I didn't recognise at the time. At any rate, he was never able to regain the weight he lost, despite liquid dietary supplements ordered by the dietician.

At the end, he had wasted away, and there was literally nothing left of him but skin and bones. His face was hollowed-out, his eyes, his beautiful blue eyes, stared out in his skull. I don't want to remember him like that, but rather as he was in his prime, striding along the London streets on his way to another marathon medal.

– 20 –

TRANSCRIPTS, JUNE 2021

1 June

MARIANNE: I think I showed you last time, there are kind of two prompts: the first one is where are you now. How is home life at the moment?

AUTHOR: Today is a very lazy day, well relatively so, because yesterday we had a long trip up to the hospital for what I was telling them would be a waste of time, because it was for tests that have already been done many times over. Nothing has changed, but because it was a different consultant that asked for them, we had to trundle all the way up there and spend four hours going through it all. So it was exasperating, exhausting. Anyway we've done it, and that's all part of it, closed. Nothing else needs to happen.

MARIANNE: Was this neurological testing?

AUTHOR: No, the thing about this type of dementia, the Lewy Bodies, is that it's a kind of Parkinson's as well, so there are a lot of physical problems and Bill's is that he can no longer pee. Six months ago it started. We thought it was the prostate and they gave him drugs for that, but it's not – it's the muscles. That kind of dementia affects every single muscle and he's going to be permanently catheterised. This is a bit disappointing for him because it is a bind and I've got to do it all obviously, because he can't cope with it. But rather that. We can move forward now we checked all that out.

MARIANNE: How are you feeling about that?

AUTHOR: It was what I expected, I could see that. Annoyed that they don't listen. It's as if they're a whole lot of different departments, with nobody talking to each other. There are the district nurses, who have been with us – putting in catheters, taking them out, testing him, etcetera. They obviously don't talk to the urologist who called for the test, and it's annoying. They should really talk to each other, you'd think, but that's too obvious.

MARIANNE: Okay, so you had a busy day yesterday ...

AUTHOR: Not so much busy as blinking well wasting time, sitting around, going for a cup of tea, getting back into the ward again. Never mind, it's over.

MARIANNE: I can sense your frustration!

AUTHOR: Yes, so a quiet day today. Bill is out with his carer just now. She's taking him out for a wee walk and she'll give him his lunch.

MARIANNE: So apart from the appointment, are you still having the six hours' care a week and how is that going?

AUTHOR: That's going fine. I look forward to it. It's nice being able to stay at home for it, rather than having to force myself to get out of the way because I feel as if I'm sitting there watching it and it's not fair. So this is a nice day. They'll be out quite a while, so I can sit up here or sit in the garden.

MARIANNE: You feel a bit more relaxed if they've managed to go out somewhere?

AUTHOR: Yes. They usually do go out for a walk and then she goes and makes him his lunch and that takes a wee while and I can be elsewhere.

MARIANNE: Yeah, it's a break. I had just one question from the interview before: have you more or less had the same person that comes?

AUTHOR: As a carer? She asked to come. They've got a nice rapport. Her manner suits Bill and he's pleased to have her, so she will wangle all sorts of things to make sure it's her who does it. We've had a few others, but it's her that he likes, that he's comfortable with. She's had to deal with one or two problems with him, of a personal nature, and he's quite happy for her to do it.

MARIANNE: That's fantastic. I suppose that's a relief for you?

AUTHOR: Yeah, because he's not in favour of having anyone in at all, and it was a bit of a battle to try to persuade him. He still says in the morning, 'Who's coming?' I'll say she's coming, and he asks, 'How long for?' I'll say, 'Three hours', to which he always replies, 'Urgh, three hours!' To be honest, I don't think he realises it's three hours he's had. He can fall asleep if he wants after his walk and his lunch, which is fair enough.

MARIANNE: That's great. You're looking cheerful today. You're looking really happy.

AUTHOR: Yeah, you got the venting, the ranting, last time.

MARIANNE: That's okay. So the other question is: What is changing? Is anything changing for you at the moment?

AUTHOR: We now have the dementia-friendly group meeting once a week in the gardens of the hotel and that's nice. That lifts everybody's spirits. And next week is Bill's birthday, so I'm hoping to be able to take a cake in and share it with everyone and just have a nice wee time. I think he'll enjoy that. He's certainly not mentioned his birthday. I don't know if he's realised.

The laugh was my sons both turned up last week and I made them a cup of coffee and we had a chat, then they said 'bye bye' and got ready to go and I thought, *They're just giving me more work. That's not what they're there for.* So I suggested maybe we should do something when they come. One of them said, 'Play Scrabble?' They haven't a clue! So I did suggest that maybe they could start learning how to put their dad to bed or give him a shower if, in the event of something happening to me, I ended up not being around. That was met with blank expressions, but I'll keep at it.

MARIANNE: Do you think that's a possibility that one of them would be able to help? Because I remember you saying that bedtime in the evening can be tricky. Do you think there's a possibility that one of them might come round to the idea of helping you out?

AUTHOR: I'm not sure. It would take a bit of persuading and a gentle induction, but you know Christopher did say, 'How long does it take to get him into bed?' And I said, it can take about an hour sometimes, by the time I do all the medications and deal with the catheter and all the other kinda bits. And he said, 'An hour? To get into bed?' So he's away mulling it over. Watch this space!

MARIANNE: I'll follow that with interest. That's really all, unless there's anything in particular that stood out to you in the last couple of weeks?

AUTHOR: Let me consult my social calendar! Oh, we went to the dentist. I take him to the dentist, the hygienist, and he managed that, and then we met a friend for coffee, which wasn't so successful as it's a very noisy place and with the lack of soft furnishings now, it all reverberates and was quite noisy. He found that quite hard, but he was cheered up because we passed the Turkish barber and he went in and had a haircut and a trim of his beard, so he's looking much better and he felt good after it. So little things like that are opening up and we're able to do them.

I wasn't quite sure how he'd manage in cafés and restaurants. We haven't got round to that yet, but when we were on the way home from the hospital, we went into a retail park and managed to go into a café for a very late lunch and he managed that. So that's a step forward because sometimes eating is very messy and he drools and some people might not like that at a table next to them. But fortunately people on either side were both disabled in one way or another so … I shouldn't laugh.

15 June

MARIANNE: How are things at the moment? How is life at home?

AUTHOR: Up and down a wee bit. Last week was Bill's birthday, which coincided with our dementia group meeting out in the hotel gardens that we do every week. So I decided I would take a bit of cake along for the group, but didn't tell the group, and I didn't tell Bill. Actually it was my neighbour that made the cake because she started up this wee business in Lockdown, and she supplies to cafés, and so on. She made this beautiful Victoria sponge laden with cream and strawberries, etcetera, and I took it along. My friend, unbeknown to me, had let the cat out of the bag, so when we got there, there were balloons and cards and some things. And then our two sons and their partners turned up as well, so Bill was really moved, he was really touched by it all, and it was lovely and the cake was delicious.

MARIANNE: Sounds amazing!

AUTHOR: The hotel provided knives and forks and plates for those that wanted them. Yes, it was a lovely day. We enjoyed it.

MARIANNE: That sounds really good.

AUTHOR: But over the weekend there, I got really tired. On Sunday I got up, got Bill up and dressed and fed, and had to shower myself. I got my breakfast, and then I just went back to bed. I could not keep my eyes open. I think he wondered where the hell I'd gone to. I could hear this wee voice outside the bedroom door calling me, but I just ignored it.

So I decided that yesterday I would contact the day centre because they'd been around during Lockdown to see how they could help, but we didn't take them up at that point. But I do feel I need a bit more of a break somewhere. I mean six hours it's not very much. But I'm not sure. And unfortunately, they are very limited to what they can do with people with dementia. I think they take four at a time or something, but they said they would keep me in mind. Hopefully, they'll come up with something, because it looks like they've got quite a lot of fun things. They've got this special bike, where they put somebody in the front and ride them round the town. And they have various activities. I think he'd enjoy it once he got used to it. He's very nervous about going anywhere different and I think once he got to know people, he would enjoy it. I hope so.

MARIANNE: I remember you said that Bill was always very active, so maybe those kinds of outdoor activities would suit him quite well.

AUTHOR: Yeah. Though he's slowed down. His walking's got a lot slower and he walks with a stick now. But for his birthday he got one of these watches that plots your route and tells you how quick you're going. He did have one before when he was a runner, but that has gone the way of all things. So this is a new one so he and his carer studied how you set it up and get going.

MARIANNE: They measure how many miles it travels?

AUTHOR: It measures distances, with a lot of wee rests, and you can see on the graph where they'd stopped and had a wee drink. It's something that keeps him occupied, gives him something to think about. My son, who lives round the corner now, commented that when he comes over and anybody else comes, Bill is much more active and aware and enjoys the company. It does make a difference having people in and around him.

MARIANNE: Are you feeling annoyed about the restrictions? Although I think the restrictions have been lifted for the time being. Has that made a difference then?

AUTHOR: Not really. Because the things we used to do – like we were members of a lunch club that used to go out for lunch once a month – I can't take him to that now. It's not running anyway, but he wouldn't cope with that now. He finds it difficult to eat a lot of foods because they're too hard. He can't manage chewing or the manipulation of cutlery and all that, so that's out. We've been going out for a cup of coffee and a bun, but that's the limit. And going anywhere with him requires such an effort on both our parts – getting him ready and into the car and away. Sometimes I wonder if it's worth it.

MARIANNE: So you're thinking that maybe if you can get Bill a place in the day centre, whatever it is they can offer, that you'll probably go for that?

AUTHOR: Mmm.

MARIANNE: I remember you spoke before to the in-home care people about having evening support and that it had not been a very productive conversation.

AUTHOR: No. I need to go through the Social Work Department, and I think I mentioned last time, I don't think the social worker has a clue about caring. But I'll go down this road first of all, and if it's not successful, then I will have to look at other ways.

MARIANNE: The only other question I had was if you feel that anything in particular is changing at the moment?

AUTHOR: Well, Bill's disease progresses really quite fast. From month to month I can see a difference. I'm not really aware of it at the time, but when I think back a few weeks, I do think, *Oh, he could do that then, but he's not doing it now*. He's already forgetting his sons' names, which upsets him, which he's not done before. Yesterday, he was just finishing off his breakfast and it was what we call our 'shower day'. I can't shower him every day, but I do try it as often as I can, so I said, 'You can finish your cup of tea and come on up and we'll get started,' and he said, 'Where's up?' And I thought, *Oh dear*, but then said, 'I mean upstairs! You know, the bathroom where you normally have your shower'. Just odd wee things like that. And then there's other times he's right on the ball. It's strange.

MARIANNE: So kind of coming and going?

AUTHOR: Yeah. Last night I was up with him because I heard him coughing at about 2 a.m., and one of the problems is his throat muscles don't work so he often chokes and brings food back down his nose and things like that. I could hear him coughing, so I got up and gave him some drinks, to just get whatever was annoying him down, and I think that will start happening maybe a bit more often. There was one night maybe two or three weeks ago that I really wondered whether I should ring the ambulance because it was quite bad, but I did manage to clear it. But that's something I have to be aware of.

MARIANNE: So, is there anything in particular you would say is contributing to you feeling tired? Or is it a more general feeling?

AUTHOR: It's just from the minute I get up in the morning to the minute I get to my bed at night, I'm at his beck and call. Sometimes he does let me have time to myself, but I can't guarantee it and I'm no spring chicken myself. It is hard work. I'm probably working harder now than I've done for quite a few years. I don't think people realise that if he wants his jacket off, I've got to help him with it. If he wants to change his shoes, I've got to do it. If he needs to make it to the toilet, well … he's got a catheter now so that's permanent, but that needs to be emptied and dealt with. If he wants a drink … anything that we would normally just cope with ourselves, he's got to have it done for him and you don't realise how much that happens in a day. I don't grudge it at all. I wouldn't have anybody else doing it. But it is heavy-going.

MARIANNE: It's a lot to be doing every day and to not know that you've got a break coming up. That's my prompts finished, unless there's anything else you would like to talk about?

AUTHOR: My younger son threw me yesterday. Bill was out walking with his carer and my son happened to drop in and we were just talking and he suddenly said to me, 'What are you going to do after he dies?' And he asked, 'Are you going to stay here? In this house?' And I said, 'Yes, I'm not going to move. At least that's how I feel at the moment.' But that's a difficult conversation too, isn't it? We kind of skipped out the funeral bit. Maybe that was an opening, but it wasn't long enough to get into it. But it threw me a wee bit. What am I going to do?

MARIANNE: I remember you saying before that you didn't feel they really understood the extent to which their dad needs support a lot of the time.

AUTHOR: He's beginning to because he's around so much.

MARIANNE: I remember you said the other week that you'd just been for an assessment that you'd already had.

AUTHOR: Yes, a lack of coordination in the health service; one not talking to another.

MARIANNE: That's a very strong theme, I have to say – the lack of connectedness between services.

AUTHOR: You'd think that each department would be keen to know what's going on with the patient, but it's only that wee bit of the patient that they're interested in.

MARIANNE: So, going back to what we were saying ... you think that that was maybe a beginning on your son's part of trying to start that conversation?

AUTHOR: Yeah, I think so. I think he's seen how much care his dad needs.

MARIANNE: Do you feel like that might lead him to maybe offering to lend more of a hand?

AUTHOR: Well, he's working from home, but he's got a very busy job. But it might in the evenings. Maybe, it could. Yes, it could.

MARIANNE: How do you feel about that? I sensed a bit of *hesitance*?

AUTHOR: Yeah I know. Could they do it as well as I can? They probably could do it ten times better frankly, but there's still that ... he's mine. He's like a kid, and I'm protective.

MARIANNE: Do you feel protective?

AUTHOR: Yeah, I do.

MARIANNE: I think that's really understandable.

– 21 –

EQUIPMENT

One Saturday night I heard a thud and went out into the hall. Bill was lying on his back at the foot of the stairs. He'd had been going upstairs and had gone about three steps when he'd lost his balance and fallen backwards.

He was conscious but stunned and there was blood oozing out of his head on to the carpet. I was going to call an ambulance, but I paused. As it was a Saturday night, an ambulance might not come for a while and A&E in Edinburgh was going to be busy. So I checked him over as best I could. Nothing seemed to be broken and the blood was coming from a patch of eczema on his head for which the GP had given him ointment. The scab had obviously come off.

So I got him slowly on to his feet and walked him to a chair.

On Monday, I phoned the GP who spoke to Bill and made him do various gentle exercises, as well as questioning him carefully about it all. He agreed that he was probably just bruised and shaken. I phoned the number for the local company that made stairlifts. The rep came out the next day and we had a stairlift by Friday!

But Bill was never able to use it without help. The process of getting himself on to it, putting his feet on to the footplate, then strapping himself in, pushing the lever and holding it until he got to the top was too much for this Physics honours' graduate to cope with now. He spent hours with me and his sitter practising all the stages of using the stairlift and making his way up or down. It meant that we could move him safely up and down the stairs and, once he was down, we could be sure he couldn't get up again.

He found sitting uncomfortable as he had so little body fat. I spoke to various people who suggested an armchair which had a system for raising and tilting the chair to allow him to get out of it more easily. I chose a huge cream edifice, which he could lie back in as well, and which had massage and heating elements. It arrived in two huge pieces which were put together and plugged in by a neighbour, ready for Bill to try out. It was a great success, though again, he could never remember what the controls were for, and moved himself up and down, never quite getting himself to the position he wanted to be in. But he was comfortable and the massage and heat soothed him when he was agitated.

The occupational therapist was instrumental in getting several additions to the house: a grab rail at the back door for him to hold on to as he made his way down the single step; a bar in the shower to grip; and a shower seat for him to sit on – not that he ever did, as he preferred to stand while the soap and shampoo rested on the seat for him to pick up when he needed them. Also in the bathroom was a special raised stool for him to sit at the basin and brush his teeth, or whatever.

She also brought in two wheelchairs with commodes in the seat and two devices for him to stand on and pull himself up – one each for upstairs and downstairs. The devices for standing were no use, as Bill didn't have the strength to pull himself up. The wheelchairs got some use in moving him from bedroom to bathroom, or downstairs, through to the kitchen for his meal.

We were given a hospital bed which could be adjusted to suit, top and bottom. The carers were delighted as our large king-size bed made it difficult for them to reach across and move him. It meant too that we could raise him into a comfortable sleeping position so that he wouldn't choke and it had side bars to prevent him attempting to get up out of it in the night.

Eating became a problem. He chewed very slowly until he was able to swallow. Meanwhile the food got colder. Rubber plates heated in the microwave helped a little, but it was quicker to reheat the food where possible. He couldn't cut his food so I did it for him, till eventually we went on to softer food that he could just spoon up. Eventually, at the end, I fed him. It was all a messy business, so I bought a roll of plastic aprons which I also used upstairs when he was brushing his teeth. He had always been very particular about his teeth and spent ages every morning removing plaque and food debris with a variety of dental brushes, floss and an electric toothbrush ... until he couldn't.

But the most successful piece of equipment was his walker, again from the occupational therapist. You see them often on the street, pushed along mainly by pensioners. They have a seat in the middle which can double as storage for some shopping. Bill and his sitter would go out around the streets, pausing every now and again for a seat and a drink of water, the bottle of course being stowed in the walker.

All this equipment took up a lot of space in the house. And then there was all the incontinence equipment: boxes of catheters, urine-collection bags for both night and day, packets of incontinence pants, disposable gloves, wipes and plastic disposal bags.

But it all helped to keep him at home for just that little bit longer.

– 22 –

FALLING

Before Bill's diagnosis, it had been me who was prone to falling. In Disney World, in 2013, I slipped on the wet boardwalk (it had been raining) as we went for breakfast, knocking into Bill, who stepped aside to save himself and left me to end up on the ground. I didn't seem hurt, but wasn't inclined to get up, refusing offers of outstretched hands to pull me to my feet. A passing nurse on holiday suggested I phone an ambulance as she could see what I'd done to myself and eventually the paramedics arrived. I was pushed through the hotel lobby on a gurney, flushing with embarrassment and giving a royal wave to everyone.

At the Disney Celebration Hospital an x-ray revealed a broken hip and I was transferred by ambulance to the bigger hospital in Orlando. Bill got to ride up front with the driver, which was almost the best bit of his holiday.

Of course, before anything happened, we had to produce our travel insurance and a credit card. The surgeon came to see me before my operation, saying that he would just put in a new ball in the hip socket which would last me 15 years. He must have seen the expression on my face because his next question was, 'How old was your mother when she died?'

'Ninety-four,' I replied.

'Oh, well, in that case, I'd better replace the socket as well,' he said.

My next fall was outside my house when I was heading out for my twenty-minutes-round-the-block exercise, a habit I had got into when recovering from my new hip. I was fiddling with my radio that I like to listen to on my walk, tripped over my feet and planted my face on the tarmac. A couple of neighbours came out as I lay there and helped me into the house. A trip up to A&E diagnosed concussion and a night when I was woken every so often to check I knew who the prime minister was.

To my shock, the next day the nurse said that as I was 70 years old they had to offer me a care package for going home. I stood straight up and said that I'd been at the top of Cairngorm the previous week and didn't need one, omitting to say that we'd taken the funicular up the mountain.

And then, one day walking into town, I tripped again, but this time managed to put my hands out to break my fall, so no damage was done.

It was Bill's turn now. On our trip across the Top End of Australia in 2016 he was on a cliff walk with some of the group. It was pretty treacherous and he was watching carefully where he put his feet. So much so that he didn't notice an overhang jutting out over the path and walked straight into it, hitting his head and knocking himself backwards on to the ground.

His first fall at our new home, after we moved to be closer to our sons, was when he was out running. Not wanting to be overtaken by a young runner at the end of their 6-mile run, he accelerated, but tripped and smashed his glasses into his cheek. Up to A&E we went to get his face stitched.

Eventually, dementia began to take hold and he became unsteady as his muscles refused to obey orders from his brain. One morning, he called for me and I found him clinging to the side of the bed as he'd tried to get out of it. He was right next to the chest of drawers, but I couldn't lift him enough to get him on to the bed, so had to slide him slowly on to the floor. I tried to pull him along the carpet on to a clear space of the floor where, between us, we might manage to get him up. But no. It was early morning and, at that time, we hadn't yet got morning carers in, so I had to press the alarm we'd been given and call the emergency carers out. The two of them had him back into bed within minutes, whereupon I then had to start the daily routine of getting him up and dressed.

Falls became more frequent as dementia took hold. I could never manage to get Bill up on my own, despite him being slim and not heavy because of the weight he'd lost. The problem was that he was unable to help himself and me. I asked my neighbour one day to help. I called my son away from his working at home. And I waited for a carer to arrive on other occasions.

When he was in respite care at a nursing home, he got a fright on finding someone else in his room and fell because of it. In the house he took to using his walking stick to get from room to room to keep himself steady. This was a man who only two years before had been out running.

The deterioration was fast and sharp.

Every week it seemed, something else would fail.

– 23 –

TRANSCRIPTS, JULY 2021

13 July

MARIANNE: How are you this week?

AUTHOR: Fraught!

MARIANNE: Okay.

AUTHOR: We last spoke at the end of June, right? And on 3 July, on his way up to bed, Bill fell backwards, down about three stairs, and landed on the crown of his head. He's got sore bits there, so he scraped off all the scabs and there was blood everywhere. He hurt his neck, hurt his back. I checked him over immediately, but I didn't want to spend Saturday night up in A&E in Edinburgh, so I just assumed he was fine, cleared up the blood, checked everything as well as it could be, put him into bed with some ibuprofen and paracetamol. The next day was actually my birthday so the two boys were here and when they came, he'd been sitting in this armchair, had his breakfast, etcetera. And when they came he wanted to get up, but he couldn't move. So the two of them had to haul him out and straighten him up, then one of them took him for a walk and loosened him up.

But we were concerned by his stiffness, so I contacted the doctor and he did a check over the phone asking Bill, 'Can you put your hands above your head? Can you put your hands behind your back?' He was fine. The doctor says it's probably just muscular, to keep taking the ibuprofen and what have you. Then I thought that moving him around was getting difficult, especially going up and down the stairs. I was having to follow him and put my hand behind him so we are fortunate here in that there is a local stairlift company and by Friday, it was installed. So we have a stairlift.

MARIANNE: Wow!

AUTHOR: Except ... he can't follow all the instructions because of his dementia. It's too much for him. We've got so far as sitting him down and putting the seatbelt on and he can press the button to go up, but when he gets to the top, he's got to do a manoeuvre to turn himself around and shuffle his feet, and that's beyond him. However, it's a great help and just as well, because a week later, the following Saturday, he fell again, this time in the bathroom. He just loses his balance and goes backwards. Nothing very serious, but it's knocked his confidence for six. His abilities at walking are diminished, I mean we've managed to walk around the block very, very slowly since. But 2 weeks ago he was recorded as having walked 3 miles or something, with his carer, in short slots. He's doing nothing like that now.

That was another thing. After his fall, the carer was due to come, but I got a phone call to say that she was self-isolating, as she'd been in touch with her brother who had Covid. So they sent somebody else for the two sessions that week. And it was someone we hadn't had before. So I had to deal with this new person and explain all the things she had to be aware of. I'd also arranged to meet a friend, so I was dashing around frantically, trying to tell her everything, trying to get myself organised. I shot out of the door and 100 yards down the street, realised I had no phone, which I needed for emergencies. Back home I came, through the house like a banshee, looking for this damn phone and eventually, of course I had to phone it. So I'm standing in the kitchen phoning my phone and it's ringing, and I'm lifting cushions looking for this phone, when the carer came up and patted my bum, and said, 'It's in your back pocket'. I'd been carrying it with me all the time.

The new carer did fine considering she had to walk into this and deal with it all. But the usual one is coming at 1 p.m. today, so that's why I'm quite pleased to get in early here [for the interview], as I'll have to start explaining all over again how the situation has changed.

MARIANNE: Yeah.

AUTHOR: But I feel I really need more support, so I've phoned the [local authority Social Work Department] and the occupational therapist is coming out tomorrow to have a look around the house again and see what other supports [they can offer]. And the social worker is also hopefully getting in touch to discuss further help. When Bill awakens in the morning his muscles don't work, they're flaccid. So to make them work, I have to get him into a sitting position with his legs on the floor. I have to haul him up because he can't. He doesn't weigh very much and he's so fragile, but my back's going to give out.

MARIANNE: You could get hurt.

AUTHOR: Yes, I'm concerned about that and I feel I need somebody younger, stronger and more able to get him up and working, get his muscles going. So I'm asking for more help in that way too. So watch this space.

MARIANNE: Hopefully Occupational Therapy will have some ideas or some resources for things that could help with that as well.

AUTHOR: We've had them out before and they gave us a handle for outside the back door and a shower stool and a back rest, because he was threatening to choke if he was lying flat, so we had to get him more sitting up when he's sleeping.

MARIANNE: How is the sleeping going at the moment?

AUTHOR: Well, he gets a pill from the doctor.

MARIANNE: It's going okay?

AUTHOR: He was awake this morning, which was surprising because normally he's drowsy, but he was alert and ready to go. Where was I? My mind's not functioning.

MARIANNE: It's okay. We were just talking about kind of getting a bit more support to get Bill moving in the morning.

AUTHOR: Ah, yeah. He's walking with a stick now inside the house as well. We've been trying to work with him, to show him how to put his weight on to a stick, because he was waving it around before and not leaning on it. My son, Christopher, is very good, very patient and gives him some instructions on how to do things, and Bill is inclined to listen more to him than to me. But we're all concerned about the future really, where we go. This has been such a sudden step down in ability. Things are coming at us apace, which we don't expect.

MARIANNE: How are you feeling generally?

AUTHOR: Och, not great, not great. I'm looking forward. I've got the sitter coming today and I've got three hours, and part of me just wants to lie in the bed and read. But I think I should get out and do something.

27 July

MARIANNE: How are things this week?

AUTHOR: I have hot news! We had the physio and OT [Occupational Therapy] people out, and they suggested a variety of things, and they said that they'd asked for me to have support in the mornings from a carer. But it wouldn't be for quite a while because they were very short-staffed. But on Monday there, I got a phone call saying, 'It's starting tomorrow' – on Tuesday. Yesterday! And it was our regular lassie that came and she was allocated half an hour each day, and twice a week, three-quarters of an hour to shower him. But in the morning she would get him up and dress him. However, after the first morning, she said that half an hour's not nearly enough time because Bill is very, very slow and getting slower. So she's put in for three-quarters of an hour every day and an hour for showering. So when she came today, we took the showering between us. She did half an hour and then I took over and finished him off. Next week she's on holiday and it will be somebody else and by the time they get it all sorted out, she'll be back from holiday But at least my foot's in the door and I've got it started.

MARIANNE: That's a start. And also that's great that you managed to get the same carer again.

AUTHOR: Yes.

MARIANNE: That's quite unusual, but really good.

AUTHOR: She put her name in there for it. She's very keen that she does it and she certainly knows him well and they like each other.

MARIANNE: That's such an advantage. Is that five days a week? Seven days a week?

AUTHOR: Seven days a week, plus six hours, letting me out. Respite care as well. I was hoping when I speak to the coordinator, if the three hours' respite care can be added on to the three-quarters of an hour that she's here in the morning, it would give me just about the whole morning.

MARIANNE: So you can just get up and do your own thing.

AUTHOR: Yeah, go or do whatever I want to do, but we'll wait and see. But it certainly is a step forward and just as well, because Bill has deteriorated again quite a bit. His walking is very poor now, very poor. I can see the need for a wheelchair shortly.

MARIANNE: Okay.

AUTHOR: Which from a year ago, when he was out jogging, is a tremendous deterioration, but they did say to expect it. That's all about the carers. I've also purchased a fancy chair for him because he couldn't get out of chairs or couches, so it's one that will tip him up when he's getting out, or it will recline him. It's got massage and heat and a bottle holder, cup holders.

MARIANNE: Very nice! That's good, and it's maybe another thing that can keep him independent for a little longer.

AUTHOR: He couldn't get comfortable because his back and neck have been so sore from his falls, but it's easing off now. The doctor has given him stronger painkillers, codeine, and that's helped. He's not taking so much now.

MARIANNE: How is Bill's balance and things like that?

AUTHOR: He walks with a stick when he does walk, but most of the time he needs support. His neck is bent, his head is at about 90 degrees to his body, which is very painful across the back of his neck, and the physio is trying to give him exercises to raise his head. And it's coming, but slowly. He doesn't understand at the moment what I'm doing with you. He's already downstairs. I put him in front of the TV with a programme he likes. He doesn't understand why, what I'm doing, or anything, so if you hear a yell coming up the stairs, he's got fed up again and is wondering where I am.

MARIANNE: Yeah.

AUTHOR: He's quite clingy, doesn't like me out of his sight, or somebody out of his sight.

MARIANNE: So one of the things I was going to ask you about ... you said you felt like your sons might be getting closer to a point where they might be able to lend more of a hand, but possibly not at the moment. [*They both had Covid.*]

AUTHOR: No, though the other one has taken over, because of the email disruption [an IT problem the previous week]. He was here on Tuesday anyway and he's coming up again tomorrow.

MARIANNE: So, you're seeing a bit more of him.

AUTHOR: He's been coming in the morning, which is when things happen, because the afternoon, we're all kind of flopped. So he's been seeing life with his dad as it really is, and I think he's been quite horrified really. He's quite shocked.

MARIANNE: When we first spoke, you just had this wee bit of support and things were kind of trundling along, but I remember you saying that you felt that things were starting to change quite quickly at that point. And right enough, it seems like things have changed quite quickly and things were quite quiet. And then all this stuff.

AUTHOR: Yeah, it was the falls that triggered it.

MARIANNE: How are your interactions with the Social Work Department and things like that? Do you find it quite easy to ask for the things that you want or you feel that you need?

AUTHOR: I'm not really sure how did I get hold of them. I did phone up the Social Work Department and they put me on to OT and Physio and it was through those two girls that we're getting the help now because they reported it. The physio is coming over once a week just to see Bill and is helping with his exercises. But I suppose it would be through them again if I needed more. But now that I'm in with the support, I feel it's easier to get the extra help once it's started.

MARIANNE: So now that those things are established, you can ask for more?

AUTHOR: Yeah.

MARIANNE: How would you say that it feels for you when you look at your life and the people who are in your life at the moment, and the different roles and things that they have? How would you say life feels generally for you?

AUTHOR: It varies dramatically. I mean, this morning we were out at the carer group and it was good fun, we had a lot of laughs, I was feeling good. But tonight, probably by teatime or thereabouts, I'll be very frustrated at Bill because he's not understanding what I'm wanting from him, or he's accusing me of doing various things. In fact, exasperated. I said last night, 'I am really exasperated with you', because the simplest thing, like walk towards me, or sit there … nothing happens. So it's a very slow process to get him to do anything or understand what's happening. And yet other times he can come away with really quite insightful comments, so you never know quite where you are.

MARIANNE: So you're still on quite a journey, I think. I remember you saying that things change when you don't expect them. It's like the idea that that the consultant had said to you, 'Well, you can expect this and you can expect that', but then what you're actually experiencing, those changes … it's a different story.

AUTHOR: Yes, and I can't get into a routine because there is no routine. It all changes so quickly. I mean, there was a wee while there, when things were quite calm, and I thought, *Oh, it's quite good, must be in kind of remission or something*. Then all of a sudden it's all blown up and it's all different.

MARIANNE: Do you feel happy with the level of support that you have at the moment, or that you'll have over the next couple of weeks?

AUTHOR: Yeah, I do. I think they've pulled out the stops to get me what I need, because I do know they're short-staffed. I mean the only reason I got this was because somebody died on [the carer's] rota and that's how I got that place. But if I hadn't blown my own trumpet, I don't know if I'd have got it. Maybe it might have gone to somebody else. So I'm afraid if you want anything, you've really got to stand up for yourself.

MARIANNE: Do you feel that you have to do that? Or that you had to do that earlier on?

AUTHOR: I had to do it all the way through, but I'm like that.

MARIANNE: Assertive.

AUTHOR: Yes. I mean when he was diagnosed at first, I was straight on to Google and looking up what I could get and what to do, and the groups to get in touch with, and all that kind of thing, and trying to find out as much as possible and learn about what he had, although he wasn't diagnosed with Lewy Bodies at first – it was just Alzheimer's. Meeting the group that we were at this morning, it's been very supportive and I know I could call on many of them just to talk to them, or cheer me up, or console me – whatever I need.

MARIANNE: That sounds like a real bonus, to have that wee community.

AUTHOR: Oh yes.

MARIANNE: To have people who probably understand much better than everybody else.

AUTHOR: Yeah, I mean they're all at different stages. Like one lady whose spouse died a couple of years ago. So anything I say I'm going through, she's 'Oh yes, I remember that', and she'll give me advice. Another one, her mum is just going into a home. There's others we met two years ago when Bill was diagnosed with dementia, but are still very articulate and understanding, and I realise how far Bill has deteriorated when I compare him with them, because at first you wouldn't have known he had it. But suddenly he's gone shooting past them all in terms of illness.

MARIANNE: I think that's really down to the type of dementia that he has – the Lewy Bodies.

AUTHOR: Yeah.

MARIANNE: Do you have any particular hopes or fears at this point?

AUTHOR: You know what's going to happen, how soon it's going to happen ... I don't know yet, but it won't be long, I don't think.

The thing that really annoys me is the need to join up all the different organisations. If there was an umbrella organisation that could take you through all the different stages and approach all the different organisations from where you need help and support – as in there's one phone number for this and another phone number for that. I have so many phone numbers and email addresses and things that I think, oh god! I've got one person bugging me about the council tax because of Bill's disability. It could take my whole life trying to get that organised and all the paperwork involved. I just feel like saying, 'Oh, bugger this! I'll just pay the blinking council tax and never bother because it's just one other thing that I don't really want to have to deal with.'

MARIANNE: Someone else described it as feeling like they had taken on another job.

AUTHOR: Oh yes.

MARIANNE: You know, arranging not so much the actual care, but the communication and the arranging of everything, and making sure everybody knows different things.

AUTHOR: And they don't tell each other! I mean I've got district nurses, physio, occupational therapy from two different sources, and the GP. They don't seem to communicate. And then all the other consultants we've seen and tests that we've had. By the time the GP gets the results, they're weeks out of date.

MARIANNE: I remember when you had to go up and do the assessments again that had already been done [by another consultant].

AUTHOR: Yeah, except that nobody had reported it.

MARIANNE: But that's definitely something that comes through very strongly from everybody that I've spoken to. I'd like to use your word from earlier, *exasperation*. Just having to repeat information and having to explain the same things to people.

AUTHOR: Eventually I typed out details of his illness, all his other physical conditions, a list of his drugs, next of kin and all that. And I just hand it to the people I'm dealing with – 'Look, it's there!' – because I was fed up going through it all.

– 24 –

WHO AM I NOW?

Carer

Believe it or not, despite my exhaustion, I found it difficult to hand over aspects of Bill's care to the carers who came to the house. I felt they couldn't do it as well as I could, that I knew how he liked things done and I felt that they had their own ways. Despite my copious (and probably annoying) instructions, they weren't as good as me.

This was brought home to me when he went in for respite care in January 2022, before he died. I was desperate, exhausted beyond belief and crying out for a break. So he went for a week to a care home on the coast. When I visited towards the end of the week, he had the wrong glasses on. He thought we'd put him in there and left him for good, and I could see he wasn't comfortable. I was torn between taking him home there and then, or leaving him to finish the week while I continued to rest.

Wife

Marriage should be a partnership of equals. Throughout our 55 years together, that changed, swinging backwards and forwards as circumstances dictated. But we always came back to the centre. But the centre could not hold any longer. I was his carer, no longer his wife, and he was unable to function in his role as a husband. He was an invalid, unable to care for himself any more, far less care for me. The pendulum swung and stuck there. Neither of us was happy.

Then when he was unsure who I was, and asked how long I'd worked there, it was the end. He still remembered my name, calling it out in the early hours of the morning, wanting me to get out of bed and go to him. Sometimes I climbed into bed beside him in a vain attempt to comfort him, or at least to get him to go back to sleep. Sleep, or the lack of it, became all-consuming to me. It was worse, so much worse, than having a young baby, when at least there were redeeming features: the baby's smile, its smell, its simple needs and the knowledge that eventually it would pass and the baby would grow up and away from such closeness. Now there was only the inevitable end ahead, looming closer and closer.

Writer

I dried up. What could I write about? I froze when it came to our situation. But I could talk to a sympathetic listener. So I talked to the Ph.D. student on Zoom, every two weeks for an hour. This went on for six months and was recorded by her in over 100 pages of transcripts.

I didn't have time or energy to write. My writing friends and contacts disappeared. Markets disappeared. But it was dementia that brought me back into writing articles for the *DementiArts* magazine produced by the Festival Theatre in Edinburgh. Plus, a wee job, after Bill died, to help with the podcasts they were starting up: I was to interview people with dementia who participated in the theatre's activities for dementia, or who worked in the theatre and ran those activities, and who would make good interviewees. I was to find angles for the presenter to pursue.

Then I started gathering all the parts of my and Bill's own journey together through dementia: my memories, the transcripts, letters from consultants, dates of hospital visits, tests.

Social animal

Covid didn't help. It masked our situation, by being confined to barracks. It didn't matter if *we* couldn't go anywhere. Neither could anybody else – apart from those in the higher echelons of Government apparently. Our social interaction was limited to brief doorstep chats or across the road, or video calls with friends and relatives, once we all managed to set up the necessary technology.

Home owner/occupant

It was as if I was only the landlady or manager of my home. People came and went – nurses, carers, doctors, even consultants, physios, speech therapists, people from dementia charities wanting to help, council workers to install grab rails or supply equipment, dieticians.

Being in control

Dementia rules okay. We were subservient to its demands and posturing.

Finding new roles

Bill's death left me bereft and anxious, lacking in confidence, without a plan or a route to take through life. It took weeks and months to shake off the tiredness. Days spent lounging about, idly watching TV, reading or pottering in the garden. And at the end of each day there was very little to show for it. I would cry at the slightest thing – a remark on TV, a paragraph in a book, a kind word from a friend – all of which I realise is part of the grieving process. But that's exhausting too. When I found myself laughing or enjoying myself waves of guilt would flood me, now that Bill wasn't there to enjoy it too.

I would worry about going out, even to the supermarket. And driving was a problem. I hadn't driven much when Bill was ill, only to appointments at hospitals, or down to the beach when the sitter was in and I was desperate for a change of scene.

I couldn't imagine going somewhere overnight, going on holiday, being away from home. I needed the security of familiar surroundings as I came to terms with my new situation.

The Ph.D. student published a paper about how carers are left in a subliminal position – neither one thing nor another, not very much in control of anything in their lives, battered hither and yon by situations out of their control, and by organisations and people who were concerned with their targets. And with a lack of facilities that offered what was really needed.

I continued to attend our dementia singing group, where I knew that people there would understand only too well how I felt, and who gave me gentle guidance on how to proceed.

My cousin had lost her husband three weeks before me, so we talked constantly on video calls, sharing our feelings and fears. At first, that three-week gap seemed large between where she had reached and where I was, but gradually, as time went on, the gap narrowed and I soon found myself catching up with her.

Our approaches to our grief were different but satisfied us both and helped us both to get through it all and emerge battered, but getting there.

Our wedding December 1966 with Linda, one of our witnesses.

Toronto 1970. Bill with Istvan in our sparsely furnished apartment.

Me watching Teddy Kennedy being interviewed outside the Capitol building, March 1971.

Bill standing outside the front door of the White House, March 1971.

Kotzebue Alaska, July 1971. Inuit children.

Adelaide, Australia September 1971. Me outside the Immigration hostel.

Penola South Australia 1971. Our new home with resident grass cutters.

Our friends Trevor and Sandy at the Blue Lake, Mount Gambier 1972.

Maureen and Barry joining us at a fancy dress party in Penola.

Another form of entertainment! A bottling party in full swing.

On the way home to Scotland 1975. Masai warriors in Kenya.

1993 Niagara Falls. About to go on the Maid of the Mist with our sons.

Camping somewhere in Ontario with Istvan's tent 1993.

Yellowstone Park, Wyoming 1993.

On top of Beartooth Pass Montana.

Mount Rushmore, South Dakota.

On our travels after Bill retired. Dressed up in Tokyo 2015.

Bill's running medals and trophies.

Our Golden Wedding at Dumfries House, Ayrshire. December 2016.

Bill with our sons outside our new home in East Lothian 2019.

Bill and his brother Neil along with Ronan and some new Australian family 2016.

Ronan and Julie's wedding in Iceland May 2018.

Bill and his pal John from the dementia singing group at the Maitlandfield Hotel 2021.

Nearing the end of his long journey 2021.

Bill as I like to remember him.

– 25 –

TRANSCRIPTS, AUGUST 2021

11 August

MARIANNE: How are things at home at the moment?

AUTHOR: Well, last week was the first week of carers coming in, in the morning, to wash and dress Bill. Unfortunately, my normal carer was off on holiday, so we had a succession of a different ones every day. And of course it didn't work out how I anticipated because I had to explain to everyone what the situation was, where things were, what the procedures were. I was being very overprotective now I think about it, and anyway, every morning I was there: 'This is for his clothes. This is where the towels are. This is what happens ...' Blah de blah de blah. An interesting mix of people came. There were some highly efficient ones who got through the work far quicker than the time allotted, but they were somewhat missing in social rapport, let's say, which would be difficult for somebody who is living alone and doesn't have people in. I think the chit-chat is very valuable for many people, but I know Bill enjoys it anyway.

Some felt quite intimidating. One said to me, 'He had a very dirty bottom this morning.' And I thought, *Oh, is that my fault*? Then I thought, *No, it is not*.

Another one came in and looked round and said, 'It's an awffy big house for the two of you. Just the two of you?'

I immediately started saying, 'It's the smallest house on the estate.' Then I thought, *Shut up*! *Why is it any business of hers how big the house is*?

But others were just lovely and really very kind and very understanding. They went through the work, didn't worry about the time and were good. But there was one day we had a new carer, and the carer's boss came in to draw up the new care plan, which took ages and the paperwork was dreadful. Then one of my sons arrived and I sent him out to cut the hedge. Then I got a Tesco delivery and a Royal Mail delivery. And then we had the occupational therapist and the physiotherapist. And I thought, at the end of that day, *That'll be it*. Then I noticed his catheter was blocked, so had to phone up the district nurse and get her out as well, to replace it, and I thought, *My house isn't my own*! And that's true, because our house is kind of a hospital ward now because we've got so much equipment stacked and stored here, there and everywhere, and people come in and they get to know the routines. The carer that was here for maybe the second or third time knows how to make a cup of tea and get Bill his lunch, so what am I running here? It's not my home anymore! There's no privacy.

Also, it was a different sitter and because Bill's walking has really deteriorated, he can't do that now. So they're confined to the house as well, especially as the weather is changing too. And I have to get out of the way. I can't get in their way. I sit up here [in my office], shut in for three hours and I found that quite difficult until I discovered a solution – nipping round to my son's and taking a book and lying on his couch for an hour or so. He works from home. I said I wouldn't interrupt him, but did he mind if I used his sofa for an hour?

MARIANNE: How does it feel when the support people are in the house?

AUTHOR: It depends. The normal carer, the usual one, we're quite used to each other, so she feels like a good friend really. At the same time, she knows how to cope with Bill, which she does very well and she knows, as I said, how to make his lunch and where the tea is and asks if I want a cup as well. So it was a relief to get her back this morning, although she's annoyed that she's no longer the sitter – she's only in in the morning.

MARIANNE: Ah, so she's swapped, and is going to do the morning, but isn't able to do the later ones?

AUTHOR: No, but we had thought, maybe if she could combine the time for the morning wash, shower, whatever, then with the three hours' respite, that would give me almost the whole morning to be able to do something like go up to the city, or whatever I wanted. So at the minute, it's a bit bitty, but they're having staffing problems, so wait till that's maybe resolved and see what we can manage.

MARIANNE: You mentioned equipment. That's the first time that you said anything about that. Is there a lot of it?

AUTHOR: We had to get a stairlift put in. We have a bed bar. There's an outside grab rail. There's a grab rail in the shower. There's a special seat not only for the shower, but also a separate one for the bathroom, so he can sit and brush his teeth. I have a huge supply of catheters and bags, and all sorts of things like that. I've also a huge supply of continence pants because he's totally incontinent. It's all over the place. Thank goodness I've got a big house!

MARIANNE: To what extent do you feel that Social-Care Services are preparing people for coming into their house? How much information do they come to your door with?

AUTHOR: Well, they do know what his problem is and they do talk. It's quite a small group in the company I'm using, so they do talk to each other because quite often there's two carers required for some patients, so the word gets around and they do know what they're coming into.

And there's also the official documentation that they can read. At the beginning, I wrote a piece on Bill's life and put it in the folder with his care plan: what we've done together, and where we'd been, and all the things that he was interested in, what he'd achieved, so they get a picture of him as a rounded person and not just the frail old man he is now. They have to write in the folder what happens when they're here and sign it, so hopefully they'll read it too.

MARIANNE: What I found in social care is that sometimes you just get told what somebody's needs are rather than *who* they are.

AUTHOR: Yeah, it's very easy to forget what lies beneath that exterior.

MARIANNE: How are things going with your children in terms of helping with Bill?

AUTHOR: The one who lives locally is good. He pops in virtually every day and just talks to his dad, does his exercises with him that the physio has set him and Bill will listen to him, perhaps more than me, because he's used to me. So he takes it on board and he always becomes more animated when the boys are here and if the two are together they're inclined to sit and chat. They were both here yesterday, quite keen to chat to each other, but I had a list of wee jobs I wanted them to do, so they kind of *humphed* about it. One was repairing the towel rail in the downstairs loo and he didn't have quite the right size of rawl plugs so he just took it off the wall and left it. So there's nowhere to hang the towels at the moment. I can live with that.

MARIANNE: A minor thing, I think.

AUTHOR: Yeah, in the whole picture of things, yes.

MARIANNE: So it sounds like in terms of service support and things, if I think back to even two months ago, there seems to be quite a lot more involvement.

AUTHOR: That's because Bill's deteriorated so much. It's such a fast, progressive disease condition, this one. We're kind of getting close to the dates we were given for the end of life. It's quite hard that, but I can see in the past month there's been a huge change in him and I can't really get used to any routine, because there is none. It keeps changing. Looking back, yes it's been a huge change and that's why we've had to get the care. The next thing will be evening care too, which I'm thinking about because that's another area which is heavy-going.

MARIANNE: Yeah, I remember you mentioning before that you thought so. This was a while ago. You thought it might be good to have evening care, but you only wanted to have it ...

AUTHOR: Yes, on certain nights.

MARIANNE: And they said, it's all or nothing. Are you starting to feel not that it might be worth it every night?

AUTHOR: It would be every night, yeah. It's the worst time for both of us obviously, because we're both tired and we're winding down for the day and suddenly I have to gear myself up to do all the things I need to do, because there's medication and catheters and all sorts of things to deal with, as well as getting him into bed.

MARIANNE: How are you feeling at the moment?

AUTHOR: Well, this morning we were at the local dementia group and that's always so supportive. We always have a good laugh. We have a good chat. We can share things and it's just nice. Going buoys me up for the rest of the week. I find Thursday, Friday, Saturday, Sunday, there's nothing really on then, so things are a bit dead. So a friend of mine is keen to come up and pop in for a cuppa. That helps too.

Oh, yeah, when I had my free time I had to go and get a load of incontinence care stuff so I just treated myself to a meal out. I had lunch out in a lovely place and I thought, *When did I last do that, actually on my own, go and have a meal out*? I don't remember ever!

MARIANNE: Did you enjoy it? Did you manage to relax?

AUTHOR: Yes, and there were quite a few single women in the place. It was so nice to have an uninterrupted meal, I must say.

MARIANNE: Good, I really admire that you manage. I suppose that you seem to be a person who grasps opportunities.

AUTHOR: I tried with Bill, when we moved here, to find everything that's going on and getting him into as much as I could. And I know I have to look forward to the future and what I will do, and maybe start preparing in a small way towards that goal. I've plenty of friends who've been through it, so plenty of people I can talk to about it.

MARIANNE: Do you feel like you're starting to feel that it's time to start preparing?

AUTHOR: Mm.

MARIANNE: In terms of the services, how flexible are you finding Social Services in terms of if you said, 'Actually I could do with more support?' As I remember, the morning support got arranged fairly quickly. So how do you feel about contacting them and asking for changes, or for more support?

AUTHOR: Well that's what I had to do before, so I know the routine now: where to go and what to ask for. It happened so quickly, even to the surprise of the occupational therapist, but it happened because somebody had died and they had a vacancy. The company is taking on more staff now, so hopefully it won't be too hard in the future to ask for some more help. And now I've got my toe in the door, as it were, it might make it a bit easier.

MARIANNE: Yeah, I think that's true.

AUTHOR: And the carers themselves can say I do need more.

MARIANNE: I do hope that a specific carer keeps being the regular visitor because it sounds to me that, particularly for you, that's been quite a key thing. Would you agree?

AUTHOR: Yes, she and Bill have a good relationship and she's bouncy and full of beans and chats away like mad, and tells you her life story and that's good for him too.

MARIANNE: Are you finding that more of the appointments and support are now at home rather than having to go out to clinics and other places?

AUTHOR: I think we're due one more clinic appointment with a urologist. It's going to be a waste of time, as there's nothing further they can do, nor does Bill want anything in the way of an operation. But for everything else they're very good. The occupational therapist and physio, they come regularly to check things. All in all, I've been really quite impressed with the help I've been given.

MARIANNE: It seems like they've been quite flexible, quite efficient.

AUTHOR: The care company, if I've got a hairdressing appointment or the dentist, I could tell them that next week, I need cover and they'll arrange that for me, and that's been good.

The new sitter is an interesting person in her own right and new to the job. I think she was stuck for things to do with Bill, when shut in the house. My friend had lent us a CD player and some CDs, and I dug out some of Bill's music from the garage where it's never been unpacked since we moved in. The pair of them had a great time, with the music turned up dead loud. And they danced – well, after a fashion – so Bill was really quite delighted with that!

MARIANNE: My only other question is, is there anything else that has stood out in the last couple of weeks?

AUTHOR: Is that not enough? It's been a hectic couple of weeks. I can tell you that I'm looking forward to a quieter life in the future. I begin to wonder who lives here? Is it just me or is it all these folks that are coming in and out all the time, taking over my house and going all through the house, knowing all the secrets of our bathrooms etc. etc.? Nothing's private any more. Then again, it's worth it.

It's difficult. We only moved here three years ago. We moved to an area we didn't know. It was the boys who said, 'It's a nice area. You'll like it.' But I knew we had to, because I was aware that something was wrong with Bill. So we started joining things like the University of the Third Age, all sorts of things, and going to various things and meeting people, doing what we could. And then Covid arrived and that all finished. And I thought, *Gosh, what's going to happen now*? So there are very few friends here and if it wasn't for the dementia group, I would be quite lost.

– 26 –

RESPITE

Towards the end of 2021, I was becoming seriously exhausted. Although I now had two carers every morning and evening, nine hours of sitters a week, and Bill had a day at the day centre, I was nearly at the end of my capabilities. Two years of increasing care and worry, endless hospital appointments and visits from a variety of therapists, lockdowns and restrictions had drained me. I had always been the one that had had health problems and now I couldn't afford to be bothered by them, though they lingered persistently in the background.

So I began to look into the possibility of a week's respite care, whereby Bill could go for 'a wee holiday', as I decided to sell it to him, and I could have a week's rest. The main respite-care facility in our area looked hopeful, though the waiting list was far into the New Year. But when it looked like a definite possibility that they would accept him for a week at some point in the New Year, they asked one question which scuppered his chances: 'Is he mobile?'

'Yes,' I answered, thinking of our slow progress round the block with his walker and his struggles through the house with the aid of his stick. 'But—'

I got no further. 'I'm sorry, we can't take dementia patients who are mobile. This is not a secure unit and they could get out.'

How far could Bill have got before he exhausted himself, or stumbled and fell, or found his feet refusing to move?

I resumed my search again. Many care homes don't take respite cases. Was it because of Lockdown and the recurring Covid outbreaks? The shortage of staff? The disruption to other residents? The lack of rooms? Whatever it was, I was drawing blanks wherever I tried.

Until, one day a home said 'yes'. It sounded okay, the reports on it were good and when I spoke to the manager, she seemed pleasant and willing to accept Bill – for £1,400 for the week. I didn't even baulk at the price. I desperately needed a break, even at that price. I also said 'yes'.

The end of January 2022 was the time agreed. Before then, I had to label all his clothes that were going with him, write out his medication requirements, his likes and dislikes around food and personal routines, and sell his wee holiday to him, with constant reminders and chats about it all. I don't know how much of it he retained. I visited the home on one of my sitter days, when she could stay with him. It was relatively new, clean and the carers were generally friendly. It was as good as any other care home.

The day arrived – a Monday. I'd shown Bill the case he would take and what I was packing for him, with everything carefully labelled, as well as a supply of continence aids and catheters and instructions. Our son, Christopher, would drive us there and help to settle him in. I felt nervous and apprehensive, I suspect Christopher did too. Bill was uncomprehending. We had planned to arrive late morning, in time to see his room and unpack, and take him through to lunch, where he could meet the other residents.

We were welcomed by the manager who left us in the care of one of her staff while she answered the phone. We were led down an endless corridor with rooms on either side, interspersed with niches holding a couple of armchairs and a coffee table. No doubt to give the residents a lay-by, as it were, to rest up before continuing their long journey to wherever.

His room was nothing special, a bit dark but relatively spacious, with a comfy chair by the window which looked out on to the car park. There was an en suite with a shower seat and grab rails everywhere and an alarm call. Bill didn't look all that impressed.

We unpacked the essentials: a clock, his water bottle and his medication, which the manager took on her return. 'We don't want anyone else lifting it and maybe swallowing it,' she said. So visits from the other residents did occur. I remembered that when my mother was in a home at the end of her life, the dementia patients would wander in and lift anything left lying about, like her special ornaments or her playing cards.

'It's just about lunchtime,' the carer said. 'We'll walk down to the dining room, shall we?'

We made our way slowly back down the long corridor. 'Are you hungry?' I asked Bill. He nodded, his concentration on walking with the aid of his stick. We'd left the walker at home, thinking he wouldn't need it. I took his arm and murmured reassurances to him.

The dining room was crowded with residents, but there was a space at the first table where three other men were seated. I helped him sit down and pushed his chair in. A carer tried to put a cloth apron over his head which he tugged away impatiently. A bowl of soup was set in front of him which he tucked into eagerly, as best he could.

Christopher and I decided that that was a good time to leave. I kissed his head while Christopher patted his back, then we said our goodbyes and left.

'Phew, that was easy,' Christopher said as we drove away. We had both been dreading that moment. Now it was over and my week of freedom could begin. Christopher dropped me home and went back to work.

I didn't do all that much that week. I was too exhausted. I went to bed when I felt like it, but still woke as usual around 6.30 a.m., in time for the carers to normally arrive at 7 a.m. I would still listen out for Bill calling or coughing, or moving in his bed. I wandered round Tesco in no hurry to return, met some friends for coffee without having to constantly check the time for getting back to relieve the sitter, went to a garden centre and wandered round the displays, all the time not quite believing my time was my own. I kept waiting for a phone call from the home to tell me he'd fallen, he'd taken worse, or he'd run away.

In the event, I phoned the home the morning after we'd taken him there. The manager said he'd had a good night – Don't they always! – but that he'd looked for his rucksack about bedtime, thinking he was going home. My heart went out to him then. He hadn't remembered what we'd told him about his wee holiday, that he was there for a week to give me a rest. I could only hope he'd settle as the week went on.

They moved him to a room closer to the heart of things as the carers quickly realised that his mobility levels couldn't cope with the long trek along that dismal corridor. On the Friday, the home phoned. He'd had a wee fall when coming out of the bathroom and got a fright to find another of the residents sitting on his bed. He wasn't hurt, but was shaken. What he was doing unsupervised in the bathroom, I don't know, as someone had always had to go with him, whether for changing his incontinence pads or simply to wash his hands. But no doubt, given his spirit, he was trying to do whatever it was himself, so that he would be more independent.

Coming out of the bathroom and seeing a stranger on his bed would certainly have shocked him. His legs would have given way and down he would have gone. How long he lay there I don't know. Maybe the stranger had enough sense to fetch a carer. Maybe a passing nurse had seen what had happened. Maybe he managed to call out, though his voice had faded as the strength of his vocal cords had diminished. The manager was very apologetic and reassuring. He would soon get over it and was eating fine and doing well.

The next day, Christopher and I went to visit him. He was wandering around in his room and we took him to sit in a small lounge nearby. We sat next to each other and I held his hand.

'I thought you'd just left me here,' he said. I held back my tears. What agonies he must have gone through imagining he was on his own, that we'd gone away and weren't coming back. It reminded me of leaving my sons for the first day at nursery and school, and waving them off.

Another resident came in and sat and chatted. She was using a walker to get around.

'My daughter put me in here,' she told us, 'after I had a fall. I'd much rather be in my own flat with my independence, rather than being here. It's all very nice, but I miss my own ways and getting up and going to bed when I want to, not when it suits the staff. I never get to watch the TV programmes I want and the TV in my room doesn't get Sky or Netflix. Too expensive, I bet.'

We took him through to the dining room for his meal and left him there, trying to reassure him that we'd be back on Monday to bring him home. Two days. Only two days more.

In the event, Christopher had a meeting on the Monday, so I drove to the home myself, arriving just after lunch. He was packed and ready to go. I took his arm as he seemed very unsteady even with his stick, and walked him out to the car, a carer following with his suitcase. It took the two of us to manoeuvre him into the car as he seemed likely to fall at any time. Getting him out of the car and into the house was far more difficult than previously. What had happened? But we made it and I settled him into his chair, adjusting it to let him lie back and putting on the heat and the massage. I made him a drink and filled up his water bottle. His catheter needed to be emptied, so rather than try to get him into the toilet to do it, I brought a jug through and emptied it as he sat there. Within minutes he was sound asleep.

He was supposed to attend the day centre the next day, but he was obviously still so tired that I kept him at home and he dozed most of the time. He couldn't tell me much about the time he'd spent in respite care. 'Was it worth it?' I asked myself? Yes, I'd had a rest, had a bit of freedom, but I can't say I enjoyed it much, concerned as I was all the time about how he was doing. He had been confused, less well cared for than he was at home, where I was there to oversee things.

Yes, I was protective, probably overly so, but he couldn't stand up for himself or explain what it was he needed or wanted done. In only a week, the staff couldn't have known all his ways and likes and dislikes, couldn't have got the measure of him, and I suspect they were coping on minimum levels of staffing. For £1,400, I could have had him in a five-star hotel, but without the personal care.

Would I do it again? Probably not. It shows the level of exhaustion and desperation I had reached that I had to put my own needs first, ahead of his. Had I known what lay ahead by the end of that week, I would have just soldiered on. Sometimes I wonder if that week in a home caused what happened next, but there's no way of being sure. Lewy Body dementia is relentless in its progress. Maybe it would have happened anyway.

– 27 –
Costs

The equipment provided by the occupational therapist was free: the walker and the two wheelchairs with commodes. The two devices for helping him stand (which were no use because of his lack of muscle strength), the hospital bed and back support, and the grab bars outside the back door and in the shower were also fitted for free by the council. But everything else we paid for.

I put in the stairlift after Bill's fall backwards down the stairs. I could probably have waited many months till Social Work or the council approved funding for it, but I felt it was an emergency. I couldn't be there every time he wanted to go up or down the stairs, nor could I guarantee his safety, even with me right behind him. We were fortunate that there was a company which made stairlifts in the town and they acted swiftly. Yes, it was expensive, but it made me feel that Bill was safer. Because he could never quite operate it on his own, by keeping the seat turned ready for moving down, it blocked off the upstairs like a partial stair gate.

I've still got it in situ. I'm not that confident that I won't need it myself at some point.

That was the main expense for equipment. Catheters and bags were provided through the incontinence service, but I bought incontinence pants for him in the local supermarket or bulk-bought them online. They were less nappy-like than the ones provided for free and, I felt, retained his sense of dignity when with a carer or out at the day-care centre. They were also dark blue rather than the white of the free ones.

I bought loads of wipes, usually in the baby aisles, for the carers to dispose of (not down the toilet!) when they'd been cleaning him up, as well as creams and lotions for his dry skin. The doctor suggested olive oil for the form of cradle cap he had on his scalp. Bill also liked to have the small, individual packs of tissues for his nose or to wipe his mouth as he dribbled, so they were scattered all around the house and in all his pockets.

I tried to make clothes as easy to get on and off and wash as possible: Primark's pull-up tracksuit bottoms with large-size t-shirts; warm pyjamas – an item I'd never known him to wear in all our married life, as he preferred to sleep in the buff; M&S jumpers (he liked them to feel soft against his skin); shoes with Velcro fastenings; a warm down jacket for his long, slow walks; woolly hats, scarves and gloves for the chilly days. He was always cold.

The armchair that moved up and down was around £300 and was a boon. He could sit or lie much more comfortably. Because he had lost so much weight, he had very little fat on his bottom, and like the princess and the pea, felt every bump and wrinkle on a seat. The heating element kept him cosy, especially with the addition of a blanket, and the massage soothed him. It sounds wonderful, but there were times when all he wanted to do was to get out of the damned thing! Again, he never mastered which button was up and which was down, so he would seesaw up and down in frustration as he attempted to climb out of it from whatever position it had stopped at.

One of the biggest costs was for the week he spent in respite in a care home a few miles from us. It was the only one willing to take him. Although the restrictions imposed by Covid had largely finished, homes were unwilling to take respite cases. And at £1,400 for the week it certainly wasn't cheap. Nor was it a great success. It was really to give me a break, which I badly needed at that time, and I did certainly get that – undisturbed nights, uninterrupted meals, no constant repetition of requests or arguments.

If I had known how little time he had left, I might have kept him at home because just a few days after he returned, he was taken to hospital and never came home again.

As a family, we had begun to look at care homes for permanent admission as we had realised that his needs were becoming too great for him to remain at home much longer, even though we really did not want to go down that path. I had always said that I would never put him into a home, nor did I want to be in one myself, so we had tried our best to make it possible for him to stay at home.

The homes we approached only wanted self-funding individuals – that is, those with a house to sell or assets which would cover the cost. But £1,500 a week was far beyond what we could afford and as I would be remaining in the house, and as it couldn't be sold, they weren't interested in taking Bill. On top of that they wanted proof that Bill had two years' worth of payments to hand – around £150,000 cash.

In the event, he was taken into hospital where he was cared for with kindness and consideration for the remaining few weeks of his life by the NHS.

– 28 –

FINAL TRANSCRIPT, 26 NOVEMBER 2021

After our last Zoom meeting in early August, there was a break until November, when I had a final Zoom meeting with Marianne to look over the past six months and talk about all that had happened.

MARIANNE: Generally, how are you doing?

AUTHOR: Well, it's been quite a journey. Since I spoke to you last, Bill's needs have increased and the workload has been very much heavier. And though I was assessed as being in need of two carers night and morning, they could only give me one up until about two or three weeks ago. It was *extremely* hard-going. I would have the carer come in at nine in the morning, by which time I would have had to get Bill up out of his bed, but it really requires two people, because I would haul him up to a sitting position and then he'd fall back, because he hadn't the strength in his muscles to hold himself up. So I was really worried I was going to do my back in again if nothing else, and when the carer arrived at nine, after he'd had his breakfast, it took two of us to wash and dress him because he's so weak.

And at night I had nobody and eventually I had to start getting my younger son to come round every night, because I couldn't do it on my own. He does a lot of weights and things, so he could bodily lift Bill up and just put him in the bed, which is what I couldn't do, and get him into a position where he could sleep comfortably at night, half-sitting up. So I have to say, I really got to the end of my tether. Because this is the shortage of carers you've read about. There just weren't any and I couldn't get them from anywhere. I even had a consultant out, who's in charge of all the dementia pupils! No, *patients*. I'm getting as bad as Bill. He thinks he's back at school and he's talking about his pupils. She's in charge of all the dementia patients and she came with her sidekick, a nurse, and took us through what was happening, then looked at Bill and promised me that within three weeks they would get him into hospital for some respite care if I could just stand it till then. So nothing happened!

Eventually they put in the emergency team, which is a team of carers in our area who respond to falls. They've got the alarm system so if somebody falls, they will come rushing out. They said they would help me every night. I think they came once and managed to put him to bed. Other times, they had to leave in the middle or before they even started because somebody had fallen, so they just had to go. And in fact, it was a night when Bill was aggressive and very difficult to handle. I eventually had to get my younger son round again to kind of say to Bill, 'Look, come on'. Meanwhile the carers went off to their emergency. I think they managed to come only three or four times but only once did they put him to bed. Other nights they would phone around 9 p.m. and ask if it was worthwhile coming as they'd been delayed. But by then I'd put him to bed myself with the help of Christopher.

So the whole thing was quite disastrous and we came to the conclusion, my sons and I, that really it was time for him to go into a care home, which was not a decision we took lightly by any means. We started contacting the social worker and contacting homes. The local home is self-funded and wanted £1,500 a week and a guarantee of us having £144,000 to cover two years. I thought the only way I can get that is if I make myself homeless and sell the house. Anyway, I put in the forms for support from the council and on the very day that a care home was trying to get in touch with me to offer a place, a care package came through. I couldn't write it. You couldn't write it.

Not only did the care package come through, but the day centre phoned and offered him a day, which is where he is now, and it was Christmas and my birthday all at once. So now I have two carers coming in at 7 a.m. We get him up and dressed and downstairs and I feed him, and two carers at night between 8 and 8.30 p.m. to reverse the process and put him into bed. I still get my 9-hour sitter service during the week, and a Friday at the day centre from about 10 a.m. when the bus comes, and he'll be back just after 3 p.m.

And for the first time in months I've got the house to myself! There's nobody here! I mean, it's felt like Sauchiehall Street, with all these comings and goings. Not only the carers, but the doctors and the district nurses, and then other nurses that are to do with dementia. And it's all those people coming and going. I have no secrets in this house. They all know where the tea's kept, and there're no secrets in my bathroom cabinet. There's absolutely nothing they don't know about me. And to have a day like this, when there's nobody and I can do what I damn well like, it's just unbelievable!

But I don't know how long it will last because, as I said, Bill's still continuing to deteriorate slowly and surely, and at some point I will have to address the care-home business again. But we'll just take it day by day at the moment.

MARIANNE: I get a sense from you that there's a sense of relief that you didn't have to go down the care-home route?

AUTHOR: Yeah very much so. I didn't realise how much it mattered to me to keep him at home.

MARIANNE: So it didn't really feel like the right time for you?

AUTHOR: As one of my sons pointed out, he's not that far down the road yet. He still knows me most of the time, though there are times he asks me how long I have worked here for, and what's my name and things. But generally he knows who I am and he knows who his children are, even if he can't remember their names. So I think we need, for his peace of mind, for him not to recognise any of us so that he could go into a home.

MARIANNE: Do you feel that that would be the kind of catalyst or the key point that—?

AUTHOR: Or something drastic happening that he needs more care than he's getting at the moment. Physically, he's got all sorts of things not working right, but he's been going to physio once a week now too, which has really helped, because before he was falling all over the place and had no strength, but they have worked wonders and we've also discovered he gets very low blood pressure so he passed out one day on me and slid down on to the floor just as we were going for a walk. Thank goodness it wasn't five minutes later or he'd have been in the street! I just had to phone up my son nearby and said, 'Get round here! Come on!' And we hauled him off the floor and dealt with it. But now we know it was his blood pressure, which was very low, under 100.

MARIANNE: Oh wow! So at the moment you're having two people in the morning, two at night and then you have a day of…?

AUTHOR: Rest.

MARIANNE: The *day of rest* at the day centre. Then you also have the hours that the sitter had right at the start when we first started talking. So you still have those respite hours?

AUTHOR: Yes.

MARIANNE: So, do things feel manageable at the moment?

AUTHOR: Yes, compared to what it was, but there are times when I am still very tired and I don't think I'll get over that for a long time. I get crabby, as he keeps pointing out to me. The most difficult time is round about late afternoon, evening, when he's *sundowning,* as they call it – when he's really *away with the fairies*, you'd probably call it. And he can get quite aggressive.

That's a sign of him having a urine infection. He's just over one because he became very aggressive again and told the carers to f— off, which is just so unlike him. And we all realised there was something going on that shouldn't be, so he's been on antibiotics and that's made a difference.

MARIANNE: So if you think he's maybe got a UTI [urinary tract infection] or something, or his blood pressure is not right, how easy has it been for you to access health-care services and things like that?

AUTHOR: Well, I've got the phone numbers I need now. I've got the district nurses. It's not a secret number, but I don't need to go through 111. I've given up on 111. It's far too slow and the surgery, the receptionists, know me well enough to know that I'm not kidding them on or anything like that. My ordinary GP is mentoring trainee GPs and he put us on to one last week when Bill had the UTI, and we had another hour session with her. She was checking everything so carefully. And you don't get that; you get your usual eight minutes or whatever it is. I mean, this is just unheard of. It's really good and very supportive and all sorts of issues can be addressed then.

MARIANNE: Yeah, you can get lots of things checked out. I thought it might be interesting to revisit a couple of questions that I asked you way back in the past. One of the things that I asked you about was if you could describe your favourite part of the day and describe your most difficult part of the day. You've kind of done that, but ...

AUTHOR: My favourite part is probably at 7 a.m. when I've got a cup of tea, the carers have just arrived and they've gone upstairs to do their stuff. I sit and stare out at the sunrise and have a cup of tea and read any emails or news that happen to have come in on my iPad. That's just a wee oasis of peace and lets me come to. I mean, I spend time worrying I'm not going to hear my alarm or something and the door will be locked when they come, but it's silly, because I always do. I'm always awake for it. And the worst part is, I think, the sundowning part, late afternoon, early evening, until again the carers arrive to take him upstairs.

MARIANNE: Do you find that the sundowning just passes? Or does it just continue until bed?

AUTHOR: Occasionally he might nod off because he's really tired, and then we've got to get him up to bed at the usual time. But it can be quite a difficult time because he's not really understanding what's happening, or where he is, or who I am. And he wants to go up to bed because he knows he's tired and I keep saying, 'No, you've got to wait till they come'. That's not at the time I would have chosen. I think I'd have chosen a slightly earlier time, but on the other hand, I think if he is in his bed earlier, then he wakens up earlier and that's not much use either.

MARIANNE: That's interesting, because your favourites are almost the same, but they're the same for different reasons. Because what you said before was that your favourite part of the day was that when you woke up in the morning, and before Bill was awake, you had a little bit of quiet and I guess you've got that again. Has first thing in the morning always been your favourite time of day though?

AUTHOR: When I had to go to work, no! But yes, if I've had a good night's sleep and there's a pleasant day ahead, it is a nice time. It lets me come to a bit and not plan ahead or anything, but just be aware of what's going to be happening and be ready for it.

MARIANNE: Can we talk about another thing that I asked you before? How did you see your role at home? For instance, what was your identity in your home? Can you describe what your role is at the moment?

AUTHOR: Chief cook and bottle-washer, and carer. Myself has kind of been conflated. Everything is secondary to what Bill's needs are. Every so often I get time out and do *normal* things and it upsets me because I see what I'm missing, you know? Next week I've got three lunches out. It's just unheard of. I've not been out for lunch for ages and I've had to organise sitters and all the rest of it. And I'm wondering how I will cope with it because it seems so much compared with what I'm used to. In fact, I could have had more friends visiting as well during that week, and I put them off to the next week because I thought, *There's a limit*. Yes, I'm very much aware that my interests and my previous life have been curtailed, but it's of necessity.

MARIANNE: When we first spoke, you said you hadn't been in the mood and hadn't had the kind of brain space to do any writing, and then you picked up some bits and you were doing articles. Are you managing to do things like that for yourself?

AUTHOR: I did five articles actually, which I was quite pleased about, and I will do more if I can find some suitable customers. One of my lunches out is with the Society of Authors – the Edinburgh crowd, as it were, are meeting. I know some of them, but not as many as I thought I would. But I'm going to go to that lunch just to be out there again, to make the link, because I'm sure they'll all have forgotten about me. I've not been producing anything or taking part in much, so yes.

MARIANNE: It sounds like a kind of support you could develop, but maybe also the lessening of Covid restrictions are making life easier for you to get out. It sounds like you're making some reconnections?

AUTHOR: Yes, exactly, because I really have done very little social media. I don't post on Facebook or Twitter [now 'X'], or anything like that now, which I was quite good at doing, but I just felt no, I can't do this. It all felt so trivial compared with other issues in my life.

MARIANNE: You spoke right at the start about feeling that part of you needed to plan for the future, or to preserve or to build some life for yourself for later on, when Bill's gone. Do you feel like that's part of what you're doing?

AUTHOR: Yeah, very much so. And of course it will be different anyway, so I don't really know how I'll feel or if I will be up to it. I think the main thing will be to just recover, because I was speaking to somebody who eventually had to put her husband into a home and she said for the next six months she did nothing but read and sleep, as she was so exhausted. And I can understand that, just to let yourself recover before you take on anything else.

MARIANNE: Are your sons more involved than they were maybe six months ago?

AUTHOR: Well, Christopher, because he's now so near, had to be involved. But now that I've got the care in place, plus his job is opening up again, he can't be around so much. He's been up and down to London quite a few times and is talking about doing more of that, so in a sense he's withdrawing a bit. Ronan is wary, very wary of … I don't know whether he can't handle his dad's deterioration. He does come, but he's not hands-on. He wouldn't really know what to do. Even emptying the catheter's a no-no for him. I think he's a little more …

MARIANNE: He's maybe struggling with it?

AUTHOR: Yes, I think he is. But that's a common reaction. Some people can deal with it but many others can't. He's pretty upset about his dad's illness and the prognosis.

* * *

MARIANNE: In terms of the service from when we first started, you mostly had a carer coming in, just for the respite care.

AUTHOR: Yes, she was just a sitter.

MARIANNE: Before the showers and anything, wasn't it? Do you still see her?

AUTHOR: She left. She walked out of her job. We have a selection of carers now. I think there's about a dozen. I was writing out how many come in.

MARIANNE: Are you familiar with them? Do you feel you know them?

AUTHOR: Some of them I know quite well; others not so well. On the whole they're a most interesting bunch. You learn a little bit about them, I'm dead nosy, you know. I always ask, 'How're things? What are you doing at home?' And I find out a bit about them, probably filing it away for a future character in a story. Did you watch Ed Balls' programmes on care?

MARIANNE: I saw the first one. I haven't seen the other one yet.

AUTHOR: He's quite right: the work conditions are appalling. One of my carers has been in four days solid. She's been working from seven in the morning till ten at night. She says she has five hours' sleep and she's exhausted. She's asked the boss to try and change that so she doesn't have to do that again. They maybe get a couple of hours off during the day. They don't get transport costs. It's zero-hours contracts. It's appalling for the work they're doing. So I'm on my high horse about that!

MARIANNE: They lack funding and the lack of support, I always think, trickles down to you and Bill and what kind of service you get, how consistent the services are and how stable they are. It's a big problem. I just went through the transcripts and in the summer interviews, you were saying you felt your house was like a ward.

AUTHOR: Yes, the equipment ...

MARIANNE: Because you had occupational-therapy things and catheter equipment and things everywhere. How is that now? How does your home feel?

AUTHOR: We've got a hospital bed now, so it means we had to take his bed, which is a king-size one, and dismantle it and prop it up in the spare bedroom, which is now unusable. I've got some of our old neighbours visiting in a couple of weeks and they're going to die when they see the house and the situation we're in. I've warned them, but yes, it's totally different.

MARIANNE: Do you think it will come as a shock to them?

AUTHOR: I think they will be shocked when they see Bill's appearance compared with even a year ago. It's quite dramatic. He's gaunt and stooped and his head hangs, and he's a poor soul.

MARIANNE: Are you still spending time with the carers' group?

AUTHOR: Yes, they've all deteriorated though. In fact, one of the carers is now dying of cancer so they've all got their problems. They [the dementia sufferers] are all deteriorating and it's sad. But the carers, there's three of us, we're going out for our lunch. So yes, they've been very supportive and I can say, 'Look, this has happened', and they'll say 'Oh yes, this is what we did'. And it's quite supportive and you can talk about anything. I mean black humour is essential about all the things that you've got to deal with, and they're not shocked. It's very supportive; a good wee group that.

MARIANNE: They understand how unglamorous life can be. In terms of service, would you say that your overall experience of home-care services has been positive?

AUTHOR: Yes, this is despite the lack of carers and not being able to get the support when I needed it. I consider myself quite fortunate compared with some people and what they've got. But as I said, it depends on how pushy you are and how assertive you are. One carer gave me some good advice. She said, 'Any time somebody asks you how are you doing, never say you're fine. Never. You won't get any help. Make the most of it. Tell them how awful it all is.' I suppose she's right, because all they want to hear is you're fine, so they'll move on to somebody else. So I will say, 'Yes, things are difficult' to those I know can help me. Other lots haven't been so good; some have been a bit of a disappointment. They were recommended. They'll phone occasionally. The last time I phoned, I said I've got the care package. That was that. Crossed off. Social workers too: if they think you're doing okay, fine; but it was me who was going round all the care homes asking what the situation was [regarding bed spaces], and other carers were saying to me, 'Don't go to that one. That's not very good. It's got a bad report'. Or somebody else would say, 'That's quite a good one.'

MARIANNE: So it was all on to you then to find the care homes?

AUTHOR: Well it certainly was a big part of it yes, because of the delays. They say, 'I'll do something', and weeks pass and nothing has been heard.

MARIANNE: Was it Social Work that told you about how the funding works and stuff like that? How you find that?

AUTHOR: I've got this document downloaded from the local authority. It's so complex. I must tell you this. My older son and I were going through all Bill's financial stuff to see where we were, how we could raise this massive fund [required to satisfy a care home], and we found some BT shares dating back 20-odd years. Well Ronan looked up the share price and calculated that they were worth £85,000! I'm saying, 'Are you sure?' So he checked and whoops! The decimal point was in the wrong place and it came down to £850! For a few minutes, we thought we'd solved the problem. That's him with his fancy degrees and everything!

MARIANNE: I'm sure your heart skipped a beat there for a minute.

AUTHOR: Anyway, we laughed. What were we talking about? Ah yes, money.

MARIANNE: How you found out about the money for the care homes.

AUTHOR: Yes, the local carers' group said, 'We have a volunteer who is a financial advisor. I will get him to give you a call.' Never heard a thing. So anyway, I filled in the form for the council and they haven't got back to me either. So I don't know.

MARIANNE: So thankfully the care package turned up then. I think that being somebody who is computer-literate is a massive advantage, because if you are somebody who doesn't have access to the internet or a tablet, and isn't able to find that information, then I would imagine that some people are quite lost.

AUTHOR: Oh yes, and if not used to dealing with people, they must find it very difficult to get to the right person and meet their needs.

MARIANNE: Can you explain to me in what way the services have influenced your life?

AUTHOR: Influenced my life? They've changed it. I have a much greater appreciation of carers and what they do and I'm annoyed at their work conditions. I'm also angry about the fact that dementia sufferers have to pay for care in homes, whereas if you have another neurological illness, which might be classed as *physical,* you get it for free. It seems a very harsh division and I think that needs to be looked at. In fact, the whole care business is in private hands and it really should be linked to hospital care. They should all be the one service so you don't get the bed-blocking that they've got at the moment, which filters back down to the ambulances queueing up to get in because there's no beds, nowhere for people to go, but a care package. Remember the old community hospitals, the cottage hospitals? They used to take the kind of patients who were recuperating. Convalescent places, that's the kind of thing that's really needed. A place, a halfway house between a hospital and going back home.

MARIANNE: To give people time.

AUTHOR: Yes, they closed everything down, thinking they're better to have this system, which isn't working. So yes, it's made me more angry about things. But I don't know that I've got the energy to do much about it except moan. And that makes me guilty too, thinking I really should be doing something.

MARIANNE: Yeah, but your hands are full!

AUTHOR: Exactly! At the moment they are. Maybe later.

MARIANNE: In terms of the support you've received and things like that, if you could relive maybe the last six months or so, is there anything that you would do differently?

AUTHOR: It was a very difficult six months, particularly before the care package came in. It seems always that you have to be in a crisis before you really get support that you need. So maybe if earlier I had been ... not *exaggerating,* but just really letting them know what I was going through. Because you do try to put on a good face and people would come: nurses, GPs, health visitors.

Bill always tries to put on a good face, to be more responsive and aware, which he does with anybody. That's why it's so good for him to be in company. So they don't see him at his worst and most difficult or most needy. I suppose what I'm saying is if they'd come and walked in my shoes for 24 hours they'd have had a better picture of things.

I don't know how you'd make it different. I can't. I can't do anything about the care crisis, the lack of people, including those needing care, working in care.

MARIANNE: How difficult is it to say to somebody that you are in a crisis, or that you're maybe feeling you have to say, 'No, I'm coping, I'm okay', when maybe you don't actually feel like that?

AUTHOR: It is difficult. I'm sure we've all been there, when we've had to admit to how awful things are, because we feel a failure. You shouldn't feel like that because you're dealing with very difficult circumstances, and unless the person has also been in that position, I don't think they quite understand. As my GP said, when I said to her that I really didn't want Bill to go into a care home – we had often spoken about it and said we would never put each other into care – 'That was before you knew what caring was and what it's about and what it involved'. And she was right. I wouldn't have thought it was anything like this.

MARIANNE: Can you think of anything that will support or help you in the next six months?

AUTHOR: It depends what happens in the next six months.

Family obviously, continuing care at the level which it is, if it's not cut. Knowing there are people I can call on for help and support. I've found the district nurses to be good generally, and the GP too – I've found no fault with them. Maybe I should ask for help a bit more than I do. I was just thinking, when Bill passed out and I got Christopher round to help lift him up, maybe I should have phoned the doctor then. I knew he was okay, so you'd think I was a medical person, but I wasn't worried about him anymore and I didn't want to bother the doctor about that.

MARIANNE: Do you feel that asking for help is *bothering people*?

AUTHOR: Not so much *bothering*, just that I have made a wrong assessment of a situation, that I should know. I do find it hard, not being a medical person obviously, to assess how much help somebody needs. I was one of those mothers who said, 'You're all right. Just get out and play. Have your breakfast and a shower, you'll be fine.' Well, they survived!

MARIANNE: I was going to say, they seem fine!

AUTHOR: Yes they're okay. Anyway, because I don't know what the situation is going to be, ask me again in six months.

MARIANNE: I suppose that's been a theme through these interviews: there's a process of adaptation all the time. Things are changing all the time. You're getting used to something and then something changes.

AUTHOR: But I don't have time to get used to the change before something else has happened. And in fact, one went the other way in that the physio really helped Bill's balance and walking, and he is more steady now than he has been for a long time. So he still uses his walker to go out and I've seen him wandering around the house without the stick now, and he's quite steady on his feet, and that's an improvement.

MARIANNE: So I suppose that's something – that you come to expect less that things will improve.

AUTHOR: Yes, I don't expect anything to improve. But there again, earlier on he had trouble swallowing, he was always in danger of choking, and the consultant had warned me about that. But he doesn't have that now. Mind you, his food is all softer food, so maybe that was all that was needed to relieve the problem.

MARIANNE: I remember that was an issue in the night-time. You were waking up because you could hear him choking. Is he sleeping elevated as well?

AUTHOR: Yes, he's got a hospital bed now.

MARIANNE: So the only other question is, do you have any other questions or stories that you'd like to share?

AUTHOR: No, I can't think of anything offhand that's happened.

MARIANNE: It sounds like a long journey, a long six months.

AUTHOR: Yeah. However we'll get there.

MARIANNE: Although it's been interesting to go back through the transcripts and to listen to the interviews more recently, it's difficult. And it's unpredictable because there were times when we spoke and you were saying, nothing much is going on. And then the next time it was like, Bill's had a fall, and everything changed at that point.

AUTHOR: Yes, plateaus and then the sudden drop-down.

MARIANNE: How are you feeling?

AUTHOR: Better than I was. More aware of the outside life that goes on regardless. When we had the first lockdown, I seemed to have time to bake, to sew. I did all sorts of things because Bill wasn't as demanding. Now all that's gone. Now I don't have the time. He wants me to be around him all the time: 'Ann, where are you? Where have you gone?' I can't even get to the toilet sometimes without him enquiring as to where I am! If I go to try to cook something, he doesn't like me going. He likes somebody around him. I think he's frightened really of being on his own. Because he knows he can't cope. He keeps thinking he's back at school: 'Where's the headmaster's office? How long have you worked here?' And he calls the carers his *pupils*. 'Are the pupils coming in? What do I have to do with them?' That must be a nightmare thinking you're back at school!

MARIANNE: Of all the places!

AUTHOR: The neighbours have been pretty good. Bill and I sometimes have a wander around the estate, just a very slow circuit with his walker thing, and they'll stop and ask how he is and offer their help if we need something.

One thing I'd like to see is a named person for each unpaid carer, who will tackle all the different strands that we have to deal with and take that weight off our shoulders. Yes, I had the support of other [unpaid] carers, who've been through the system, but there must be a lot of people who could do with this named person to wind their way through that forest of administration and forms.

MARIANNE: Somebody like that would also know the short-cuts that it's taken you so long to learn. Somebody who already knows. Did you have a person through Alzheimer's Scotland who was your post-diagnosis support worker for a year?

AUTHOR: I think so. It was supposed to be a nurse. I think we saw her twice and then Covid struck. It was more to do with, 'How's the medication?' I was talking to another carer the other day and suggested they apply for a Blue Badge. They said, 'Oh she's not bad enough for that. She can walk okay.' I said that we had one, not because Bill couldn't walk at that point, but that he was a danger to himself in traffic and car parks, as he would just wander into the traffic when getting out of the car, or step off the kerb without looking. So there's the informal passing-on of information to each other, and it's just luck that you find it out.

Part III

LEAVING

– 29 –

DEATH COMES AT LAST

March 2022

His bright blue eyes stared unseeingly at me. He was dead. Gone. Nothing of the man I married was left. His wasted, gaunt body lay twisted under the thin hospital cover, his cheeks sunken, exposing the yellowing teeth and gums. He was, and wasn't, my husband. The moment had come at last. The moment I'd dreaded for so long. The moment I had half-wished for towards the end. I couldn't bear to see him a shell of his former self, a carapace of the man I'd married all these years before. I didn't want him to suffer any more. I didn't want *me* to suffer any more, though I knew ahead of me lay a long passage of time before a semblance of normality would return.

And still his eyes were open and staring at me. Aquamarine blue. One of the first things that had attracted me to him. The cliché is 'piercing' and so they were, looking into my soul.

The nurse came in and rubbed my back as my tears fell.

'I'll close his eyes,' he said.

'No,' I remember saying. 'No, don't close them.'

I wanted still to be able to look in them. To feel he was watching. To feel he was still there ... he hadn't gone.

My younger son arrived and the nurse left us to share our grief and thoughts.

I had been to Tesco that morning, picking up a few essentials before I planned to go to the hospital and see him. The night before I'd been googling signs of death and came across an article on times of death – early morning or around 11 a.m.

'I'd better get there before then,' I told myself, throwing the shopping into the fridge and setting off again. He'd been in the local hospital just a couple of days, after spending a month in the Western General in Edinburgh. It had meant a two-bus journey to visit him, but between my sons and me, we'd managed to be there virtually every day. But having him five minutes down the road was much, much easier. I used his disabled badge to park near the entrance and made my way to the ward.

I could see from the minute I went into his room that he was dying. His breathing was laboured and he was unresponsive. He'd been like that for a few days, but there was something undefinably different that morning. I stroked his head. He'd liked me to do that, finding it comforting and relaxing. And so I stroked it and murmured to him. Hearing is apparently one of the last senses to go, so I whispered some words to him. As his breaths became shallower, I phoned my son and told him to come straight away. He was working from home and in the middle of a Zoom meeting, but he dropped everything and came. Except he couldn't get parked in the hospital car park so by the time he managed, his dad was gone.

It was just a gentle stopping. A ceasing of air in and out. A long pause. One more. And then it stopped. I carried on patting his head and whispering, his eyes fixed open, unseeing … and gone.

It was 10.55 a.m.

Things moved into action then. The nurse showed us to the 'quiet room'; a place to go on such occasions as this. It was blandly furnished, more like an undertaker's waiting room. Tasteful and underwhelming. There was a kettle, cups and saucers and a supply of tea and coffee, a CD player and a selection of suitable music. Dusky-pink comfy seats and cushions. We sat there looking at each other, uttering stark phrases about mundane items. Christopher phoned Ronan, who arranged to meet us back at my house – the house my husband and I had shared, which was filled with his possessions and presence.

In that hospital room, no one came. We sat there for ages, waiting what for we didn't know. The nurse had said they would be with him, we assumed laying him out, doing the admin which goes along with a death. But when we returned, he was still lying there, eyes wide open.

I kissed his forehead and left then and we drove in our separate cars back home. When Christopher had first tried to visit his dad in the local hospital just the other day, he'd missed the entrance to the hospital and driven all the way to the coast before he could turn around and make his way back. Away from the main road, this part of the county has many country roads winding and twisting their way over the hills. To reach many of the coastal towns and villages these are the roads you have to use. My satnav took me the most difficult ways along narrow roads and hidden bends, dipping ups and downs,. Meeting anything larger than a car meant coorying into the edge of the road, trying not to end up in a ditch. But to compensate there were stunning views which would appear just as you crested a hill, turned a bend, or were glimpsed through a rambling hedge.

Even the bus, the one time we took it to a coastal town, nearly caused Bill to be travel sick, though he was inclined to panic at other people's driving. Once in China I had to work hard to stop him having a panic attack on a heavily laden bus meandering its way through the rolling hills. We had been given seats as we were foreigners, and I was glad as he hated being in a crush of bodies. So I chatted to him about the passing scenery, remarking on anything that caught my eye: a new bridge being constructed, reaching high above the road we were on; strips of paddy fields with the occasional worker bent half-double in them; workers and women on bikes, keeping well in to the side of the road till the bus passed them safely.

All I had left now were our memories built up over 55 years: good ones, rotten ones, ones we'd shared a laugh over, ones we never mentioned, ones that were special and only needed a word or a glance for us both to share the incident.

I miss that perhaps most of all. Nobody to share with.

– 30 –

LAST RITES

The next days were a haze of contacting people and organising the funeral. I made a list of friends and family and started emailing – short, sharp and to the point*: B died today. I was with him at the end. Details of funeral to follow.*

Then the ones with no email that I knew I should phone. I managed two. Not that I *managed* them, but I got through them, after breaking down the minute someone answered.

For the rest I sent wee cards. I couldn't hack the constant tears and upset that talking to people did to me. In the end I also put a message on Facebook for all those further outside the friendship circle.

I'd thought about the funeral quite a lot in the preceding months but when it came to the crunch, I wavered. What if it wasn't the done thing? What if he'd rather be cremated? We'd decided – or rather *I* had decided – to be buried in Binning Wood, a natural burial site in the middle of woodland. Anne, my friend who had started the singing group, had taken us on a walk through there when we first moved here, and I had been attracted by the peace and tranquillity of the place, and the quirky little plaques on each grave. Newer graves were mounds, but the older ones had sunk down to the level of the rest of the site and only the little plaque showed where they were.

One caught my attention. Apart from the name and date, it told us that the person had been buried alongside his beloved green iguana. I fancied that site. I searched for undertakers – there were, it seemed, only two in our town; one apparently run from a house. I chose the other. It turned out to be a huge organisation, which had supplied the hearse to bring the Queen from Balmoral to Edinburgh. Bill was in good company.

Organising the purvey – that meal that follows a Scots funeral – I had already decided that the hotel where our dementia group had met, outside in the gardens when we were forbidden to meet indoors, would be the place. But what to have? When?

Then notifying the authorities once I got the death certificate from the hospital: *Frailty*, it said, *with Lewy Bodies secondary*. Certainly he was frail. There was nothing left of him except for his piercing blue eyes. They said the Queen's certificate shouldn't have said *old age*, as it's apparently not a proper reason. She too had frailty, but nothing like as severe as Bill.

For the funeral, I had the piece I'd written on Bill's life for the care-plan folder, and the article on Bill's marathon races in *Hidden Lives*, the column I wrote for the *DementiArts* magazine put out by the Festival Theatre in Edinburgh. Even so the boys wanted to add their thoughts and memories to it, to be read out by the celebrant. So it grew and grew. In between we wanted some music. As it was a humanist funeral with not a word of religion – despite the fact that Bishop Joseph Devine had grown up in the flat above Bill in Fauldhead – I wanted music that reflected Bill's taste and life. So, 'Waltzing Matilda' for the years in Australia, Willy Nelson's 'On the Road Again', for his love of country and R'n'B, and Anne was playing her medley of 'Mrs Magpie', the song she and I had written for our dementia group, together with 'Ae Fond Kiss' and 'Waltzing Matilda'.

Marjorie, another close friend and member of the singing group, arranged the flowers beautifully: blue and yellow irises; three bunches; one for each of us – me and our two sons – for the coffin. We had cards to write our last messages on. Did I pick them up? I don't know if I have them from the burial.

The day of the funeral it rained off and on and was wet underfoot. My brother arrived the day before to stay with me.

The funeral was at 11 a.m. on Wednesday, 16 March. Our sons and their partners met at our house and waited for the hearse to arrive. I wore the dress I'd bought for our Golden Wedding. It was black with a red-and-orange top bit, so it was quite appropriate. I struggled to put a bit of make-up on as I hadn't worn any at all during Lockdown, and it was a bit dried-out. I had tights on too and wore my fancy boots with my wee black slip-on shoes to change into for the celebration of his life at the hotel.

We were having a private burial. Just immediate family at the graveside. I felt the drive in the limo would be difficult and it was. Nikki, Christopher's partner, and Julie, Ronan's wife, and I squeezed into the back seat, with the boys at the front. As we started to move off, Marjorie and Anne, our friends from the dementia group, were standing at the corner to wave Bill off. Unsurprisingly, I cried. We drove to Binning Wood, me trying not to cry too much. Nikki held my hand. We drove straight in and up to the burial ground. His grave wasn't very far in – near the iguana one.

The undertakers handled it all very well. The guy from the Humanist Society read a wee poem and did the honours, before we threw earth into the grave and made our way along the muddy path back to the car for the drive home. We were going to be dropped off there and take our own cars round to the hotel to meet the rest of the mourners, celebrate Bill's life and have something to eat.

Then the fun started. Our shoes were covered in mud. We were supposed to have a quiet ten minutes composing ourselves before heading to the hotel. But when I opened the door, my brother charged in and sat on the stairs to remove his muddy shoes, leaving mud all over the hall carpet. I took his shoes and using a nailbrush at the sink, removed as much as I could, while Christopher supplied everybody with paper towels to remove the worst of it. Julie had brought a separate pair of shoes to change into and others scraped their shoes on the grass. The humanist guy had followed us, thinking we were going straight to the hotel and was a bit nonplussed to arrive at the house.

Eventually we were ready and headed off to the hotel where everyone was waiting. I took a deep breath and a glass of white wine and went in, and the service started.

I think Bill would have been pleased with how it went and who was there, as well as who watched it on the stream we'd set up. The dementia singing group all came and some friends had travelled quite a distance to say farewell.

The celebrant read the eulogy interspersed with the music we chose, some played by Anne on the piano we used for the singing group, or on CDs.

The purvey was plentiful and we gave people doggy bags to take home the excess. The hotel organiser was good that way.

I don't remember much of import after we got back.

Everybody went home.

– 31 –

RETURN TO BINNING WOOD

Two days later, I decided to go back to the grave to have a proper look. I wanted to see the flowers and have my own quiet moment with Bill. It was early and it was dry.

It was hard to get into the car and drive myself there. I had to keep snivelling the tears away so I could see where I was going. As it was, I didn't realise there were two entrances and so I went in the first one I came to and parked. I walked along the path, hoping that the few people around wouldn't see I had been crying, and was pretty close to starting up again.

I was so concentrating on my own distress I didn't notice for a while that there was no way a car, let alone a hearse and a limo, could have made it up the narrow path I was following. Being mid-March the trees were still quite bare and only the very earliest of greenery was showing. At the top of the path I stopped to catch my breath and then realised that this was not the right road. I felt the burial area was over to my left, so I struck out on the first sign of a path heading in that direction. Eventually I came to a large pond, swollen with all the rain and looking quite attractive. But that was not my goal.

I trudged on through some muddy bits, as the ground hadn't

fully dried after the downpours. I came out of the trees and, across the road, I could see some graves. I rushed in and stopped. None of it looked familiar. Where was Bill? Where was the guy with the green iguana? I wandered among graves which seemed to be older, not so fresh as Bill's would be. How was I going to find where he was? There were none with recent flowers or largish mounds, and the site seemed to stretch all the way down the hill.

A woman carrying a clipboard approached. I went up to her and explained I was looking for my husband.

'My husband's in here somewhere too,' she replied. 'He's counting all the trees and checking them over for disease.'

'No,' I said. 'Mine was buried here a couple of days ago and I can't find where.'

She checked her clipboard. 'I'm marking where all the graves are,' she told me, 'so the owners have a record of them all. But let's go and find the gravediggers. They should be able to help.'

The gravediggers were obviously preparing to dig another grave and I recognised one of them, a lady, from the funeral. I'd been quite surprised that one of them was female, but nowadays, why not?

She actually recognised me and even remembered my name.

She took me down to where Bill was buried. The flowers still looked fresh and I thanked her as she went back to work. Marjorie had done a great job with the flowers and the three bunches were laid out along the mound. Because it's a natural burial ground, nothing plastic is allowed and they were tied with garden twine. They would be left there until they died off naturally and turned slowly into compost, rejuvenating the soil.

I relived the burial service and thought about Bill a lot and our life together. It struck me then that I was alone now, on my own, to do with my life what I chose.

– 32 –

LOOKING BACK

We received loads of literature on dementia, available resources, things to buy, where to claim for help and money, phone numbers and websites, and more phone numbers. I have files of literature and letters, flyers and pamphlets, where to go and what to do, but I have to confess I don't remember paying much attention to any of them. It was all too much to take in at first and later, my brain wasn't capable of doing so, given the endless slog of caring.

Yet there was plenty of useful information contained in them. I even found, over a year after Bill's death, sheets of information and worksheets that Bill had received early on, when he was visiting a psychologist at the hospital to help with his anxiety and the intrusive thoughts he was having. He was taught about mindfulness and Cognitive Behaviour Therapy and how he could use them to help himself. It was very useful but it stopped with Lockdown, though it continued for a short while by phone. But Bill wasn't comfortable doing it that way so that stopped too. Perhaps it would have been more helpful had the sessions gone on for longer and Bill's disease had been slower in its progression, but it faded quickly from his memory in no time at all. He also lost the ability to read and take in information. I can see from his writing on the worksheets how dementia impacted that – it's tiny and faint and disjointed.

Dementia affected every aspect of his life.

For me, the most helpful thing I found was sharing my feelings and what I had to do with other people who understood and/or had been through it all: the sessions with the Ph.D. student on Zoom, the singing group after which we had coffee and a chat. Knowing that what was happening to us had happened to others and they had survived its trauma.

The whole experience changed me. I hope I am now less self-centred and more tolerant of others, that I have more empathy and appreciation of people's difficulties, that I am a better person for having gone through it. Of course there are things I wish I had done differently but I have learned that life is too short and precious to spend on looking back at what has been. Rather move on, taking with you the lessons you have learned and putting them into practice.

– 33 –

TWO YEARS ON, MARCH 2024

The first anniversaries have all been reached: the first birthdays, his and mine; the first wedding anniversary; the first Christmas; the first anniversary of his death; the funeral. All have been reached and dealt with in various ways. All have generated their own grief and memories, their own particular heartache, their own numbness and ways of dealing with it.

The various supposed stages of grief are crap. They don't come along in a neat progression, so you can watch yourself travel along the rails back to normality. Rubbish! It's a roller-coaster, up and down and roundabout. You never know where you are or how you're going to feel. I can be pottering along happily when all of a sudden, I'll be in tears from a sliver of memory, a few words, a feeling. Sometimes it's only momentary, other times it lasts all day – and all night. The nights are the worst. The wee small hours have their own particular form of torture. Things I've said, things I've done, things I didn't do, things I should have done ... it goes on and on, berating myself for my shortcomings and inadequacies, my sharpness, my thoughtlessness.

I list what I've achieved over the first year, given the complete lack of confidence, the screaming anxiety that a bereavement leaves you with. Downstairs has been repainted by our local handyman, freshened up, and all the marks from wheelchairs and other equipment covered over in a colour – away from the off-white of a new-build's walls. The same guy has also laid a bit of decking and a path in the garden, allowing me to walk up to the patio in the sunniest bit of the garden without wet feet. All I need is some sunshine to sit there, the empty chair beside me.

I've been away. A trip to a christening on the west coast with a stay in a very nice Airbnb. A weekend at a writing conference where I met up with many friends. A Christmas trip to Christopher's new house in Glasgow, followed by a stay at my cousin's in Ayrshire. Nothing like the travels we used to do, but it's a start. I'm still always glad to get back to my home and my own bed – a sign of getting older perhaps?

I have a wee job (paid), which I was offered in a theatre in the city, interviewing people for dementia podcasts, which has been great fun and I've met all sorts of interesting characters. I've had short articles accepted for publication, and I've been out and about for lunches and coffees with friends. It all counts. Every little thing is an achievement, another step on whatever road it is I am travelling.

But grief has ways of making you suffer. My health hasn't been great: two bouts of Covid leading to eye problems, and frequent visits to a variety of hospitals and surgeries for other ailments. Mind and body in cahoots. Suddenly I feel old. In the last few years, since I began life as a carer, I feel I have aged ten years at least. I even suspect my mind isn't as sharp: I forget things, words, what I was doing, names. My energy is much lower. My balance is much worse. I'm glad I kept the stairlift, the grab rails, the alarm call – I might well need them in the near future.

On other days I'm raring to go. They make up for the days when lethargy overwhelms me and has me sprawled on the couch, a blanket around me and a hot-water bottle clutched close. For after all, energy costs have spiralled and although cold infiltrates my body, I don't feel I can put the heating on until it creeps well down into the teens on the thermostat. But even with the heating on and the house warm, I still like to have the hot-water bottle and the blanket as a poor substitute for Bill's warmth when we cuddled up to watch TV. I see now why single people have cats and dogs, for the comfort a warm and living being creates.

But I also have to acknowledge the freedom being on my own brings. I am in charge of what I do, and when. I get up when I want, eat my choice of breakfast or none at all. I go out where and when I please. If I don't feel like doing something, I can call it off, though I don't often, as I realise it does me good to be out and busy. I'm always amazed by how crappy I can feel, but after a shower and getting dressed, life can look very different. Company of people helps.

Going somewhere new is never easy. Going on my own makes it far more difficult. But having done it, it leaves me with a feeling of satisfaction, of pride even, that I can do it, that I'm coping most of the time. But I'm always glad to get back home.

The latter part of 2023 came up trumps. I went a wee break round Scotland with a friend on an oldies' holiday, I spent my birthday at the Royal Garden Party at Holyrood and even chatted with Princess Anne. And I went for a week to Hungary with Anne to meet up with Canadian friends Istvan and Eva. (Istvan and Bill had taught together in Toronto in 1969.) Istvan took us to the flat in Budapest where he'd grown up until 1956, when the Russian invasion took place and he and his family had to flee. They became refugees, eventually making their way to the UK. Having friends in Hungary meant that we had some fascinating experiences with them, like joining in the grape harvest and picking grapes on the family smallholding, teaching their children to do the Dashing White Sergeant and being overwhelmed by their kindness and hospitality.

And I wrote this book.

USEFUL RESOURCES

Age Scotland, **www.agescotland.org.uk**, Tel. 0800 12 44 222.

Age UK, **www.ageuk.org.uk**, Tel. 0800 67 81 602.

Alzheimer Scotland, **www.alzscot.org**, Tel. 0808 808 3000.

Alzheimer's Research UK, **www.alzheimersresearchuk.org**, Tel. 0300 111 5555.

Dementia UK, **www.dementiauk.org**, Tel. 0800 888 6678.

Join Dementia Research, **www.joindementiaresearch.nihr.ac.uk**.

The Lewy Body Society, **www.lewybody.org**, Tel. 01942 914 000.